BECOMING: WHAT MAKES A WOMAN

Edited by Jill McCabe Johnson

Introduction by Janice M. Deeds, Ph.D.

The University of Nebraska—Lincoln Gender Programs

Copyright © 2012

University of Nebraska—Lincoln Gender Programs
340 Nebraska Union
Lincoln, NE 68588

All rights reserved.

No part of this book may be reproduced, stored in a retrieval system, or, transmitted by any means without the written permission of the authors.

Ellen Bass, "If You Knew" from *The Human Line*. Copyright 2007 by Ellen Bass. Reprinted with the permission of The Permission Company, Inc. on behalf of Copper Canyon Press, www.coppercanyonpress.org.

Designed by Kimberly McDonald

Printed in the United States of America

10   9   8   7   6   5   4   3   2   1

ISBN-10: 0615587100
ISBN-13: 978-0615587103

IN GRATITUDE

The Editor would like to thank the following Associate Editors for their assistance selecting contributions for this anthology: Noah Ashenhurst, Nancy Canyon, Reece Carson, Robert Fuglei, Erin Hollowell, Jacob Hilton, Julie Johnson Riddle, Michael Schmeltzer, Tina Schumann, Natalie Tilghman, Juniper White, and Tarn Wilson.

Special thanks to Kimberly McDonald and Mike Jackson from the University of Nebraska—Lincoln Student Involvement Information Strategies for their layout and design work, and artist Steven Gardner for the use of "Earth" for the cover.

ACKNOWLEDGMENTS

Alaska Quarterly Review: "The Bath"
The Arkansas Review: "The BB Gun"
Best New Poets 2005: "After Ovarian Surgery"
Brevity: "Comfort Food"
Calyx: "Asceticism"
The Collagist: "Rumor Had It"
Constituents of Matter: "Moose, Looking"
Diagram: "On Not Pivoting"
Dust & Fire: Writing & Art by Women: "SiLozi Song"
Female Nomad and Friends: Tales of Breaking Free and Breaking Bread Around the World: Portions of "Getting Bombed"
Harpur Palate: "Ontology"
The Heartland Review: "Apostrophe S"
Hinge, 2006, Black Zinnias Press: "Yardwork"
Hospital Drive: "Urn"
The Human Line, Copper Canyon Press, 2007: "If You Knew"
The Los Angeles Times: "Happy Birthday"
The Missouri Review Online Poem of the Week: "Recovery"
The Pisgah Review: "Eggs"
PMS poemmemoirstory: "Passing the Cups"
Poet Lore: "Inside the V.A. Dictaphone Typing Unit, Division of Outpatient Psychiatry, 1969"
Primavera: "At the Embers"
Quarterly West: "Women Who Pawn Their Jewelry" and a longer version of "Two Mothers"
The Sun: "Heat"
Triplopia: "If Women Ran the World"
VoiceCatcher4: "Portrait of a Cowboy as a Young Girl"

CONTENTS

Introduction i

Preface ii

What Made Me – Peggy Shumaker 1

Portrait of a Cowboy as a Young Girl – Carolyn Martin 3

It Did Not Seem Odd – Sherrie Weller 4

The Language of Flowers – Bibi Wein 6

Overlooking the Blue Ridge Parkway – Tammy Tillotson 9

My Mama Cheating on My Daddy with James Brown – Keli Stewart 10

The BB Gun – D. L. Hall 11

Romance – Beatrice M. Hogg 15

At the Embers – Andrea Potos 17

Annmarie's Bear – Louise Schnurr 18

Above the Hard Earth – Susan Leahy 20

Black Cat – Marjorie Manwaring 22

Roses – Emily Levine 23

Flying: Round and Round – Jenelle Tabor 25

Pivot – Lita Kurth 29

Number One – Adrian Gibbons Koesters 32

Mon Deye Mon – Nadine Pinede 36

Eggs – Susan White 38

She Leads Me – Marjorie Saiser 42

Heat – Michelle Cacho-Negrete 43

Asceticism – Rebecca Lauren 46

Band Practice – Anne Pekuri 47

Kerosene – Julie Hensley 51

Yard Work – Kathleen Lynch 52

Title IX and Me – Nancy McKinley 53

Deal with it Madame – Huda Al-Marashi 55

Test Group Four: Womanhood and Other Failures – SJ Sindu 58

Inside the V.A. Dictaphone Typing Unit, Division of Outpatient Psychiatry, 1969 – Maria Terrone 61

The Jumper – Christin Geall 62

Passing the Cups – Elaine Neil Orr 64

Phone Call to Dublin – Kerri French 68

Ontology – Nancy J. Nordenson 69

Two Mothers – Chavawn Kelley 71

SiLozi Song – Jill N. Kandel 73

Where Do Babies Come From – Jennifer Brennock 76

Rumor Had It – Dilruba Ahmed 79

Iraq 2003: Getting Bombed – Kelly Hayes-Raitt 80

If Women Ran the World – Ellaraine Lockie 86

Women Who Pawn Their Jewelry – Sheila Squillante.................................87

Moose, Looking – Anna Leahy 88

Happy Birthday – Dinah Lenney..89

After Ovarian Surgery – Jennifer Chapis 92

You Are I – Judith Slater..94

If You Knew – Ellen Bass 98

Not Too Old – Margie Lukas...99

Apostrophe S – Jennifer Gibson..102

Trying to be Normal – Marilyn Bates 104

The Whole World's Watching – Sibyl James 109

The Bath – Holly J. Hughes...111

Recovery – Julie L. Moore 112

Hopkintown Iowa – Kay Mullen 113

Wild Love – Marjorie Rommel 114

Comfort Food – Lisa Ohlen Harris 115

Urn – Marci Ameluxen 117

On Not Pivoting – Lia Purpura..118

INTRODUCTION

Janice M. Deeds, Ph.D.

How does a woman become a woman? For the past fifty years psychologists and other social scientists have generally agreed that while sex is a biological state (male or female), gender (man or woman, masculine or feminine) is a social construct. The personality traits, behaviors, and roles associated with being a woman are modeled within the family and reinforced by the society surrounding us, including media messages that reflect the values of popular culture.

As demonstrated by the authors in this anthology, although there are common life experiences and expectations that women share, each woman has a unique set of influences from which she develops her identity. Readers will find moments of recognition and moments that surprise and sometimes challenge their perceptions of the kind of experiences that influence gender identity. These poems and stories will encourage each of us to reflect on the moments in our own lives that shaped our identity and led us to become the women (or men) we are.

Dr. Jan Deeds is the Associate Director of Student Involvement Gender Programs and Director of the Women's Center at the University of Nebraska-Lincoln. She is nationally known for her work for gender equity, relationship violence prevention, and feminist therapy.

PREFACE

Jill McCabe Johnson

Across the arc of a woman's life, significant events and rites of passage often become the public signposts of change and growth, but these transitions—graduations, accomplishments, falling in love, and physical shifts to the next stage of womanhood—don't necessarily have as much significance as the internal evolutions spurred by experience. In compiling this anthology, we asked writers who identify as women to share the pivotal life experiences that made them into the women they are today, those moments of *becoming*, when, in looking back, they had undergone some fundamental transformation that forever changed the women they were to the women they would be.

    The stories women shared, the intimacies, sacrifices, victories, tenderness, and violence, span all stages and ages of life, from early childhood to the vibrant years of later life. This anthology of poems and personal essays follows that arc of experience. Although the authors come from a diverse range of cultures, ethnicities, belief-systems, sexual orientations and identities, they share the common element of growth. They have learned from, as well as led the way for, others. They have faced doubts and triumphs, losses and joys. They are the voices of unique experience that transcend individuality to become the bonds of human understanding. With them, I thank and give tribute to all the mentors who have helped each of us become who we are today, and dedicate this book to the future generations of women who will, in turn, be the guides and architects of succeeding generations in this lone, sometimes frightening, often exhilarating business of life.

WHAT MADE ME – PEGGY SHUMAKER

Tucson, Arizona

Tracing outlines of autumn
leaves—maple, sycamore, oak—

coloring inside wide lines
scarlet, pumpkin, gold,

I wonder … Where exactly
does this happen? Autumn

in our desert means
heat lifts its anvil

off our chests, means
a bare foot on the sidewalk

won't sear. Palo verde
and mesquite beans

clack between
dusty velvet smidgens,

tiny leaves, punctuation
for twigs.

They taught us to see
what wasn't there.

Let us know what's important
we'd never seen.

What we did see
every day on the way

to our lives,
wasn't in

science books:
saguaro, ocotillo,

scorpions, horny toads,
rattlesnakes, jojoba,

creosote, kangaroo rats,
June bugs, Gila monsters,

barrel cactus
in waxy bloom…

Grapefruit and
orange groves

remained our secret
hiding places,

our hearts rich
as cotton fields

twice picked, gleaned,
disked under.

PORTRAIT OF A COWBOY AS A YOUNG GIRL – CAROLYN MARTIN

Mugging for the camera
in brand new cowboy boots,
she still insists she's Roy not Dale,
riding down the Happy Trail with Trigger
and the Sons of Pioneers.

She smoothes her bronco-busting chaps,
pulls tight her white-fringed gloves,
adjusts a broad brim hat that tilts
above her bangs straight-cut
and ties beneath a stubborn chin.

The lens clicks up the front porch steps,
corrals her closed-mouth smile,
her arms akimbo, stance girl-proud.
It's 1948. She's three,
decked out in faux rawhide.

This day, *You Are My Sunshine* plays
inside her head -- the words exact,
a bit off-key. *You make me happy…*
those straight-on eyes convey…*please
don't take my sunshine away.*

I don't recall who shot this frame,
or how it felt to roam the Jersey shore
the King of Cowboys, Son of Pioneers.
I don't recall the guns, the fringe,
the voice that sang *when skies are gray.*

I can't recall when I was more
of me than on that sunless winter day.

IT DID NOT SEEM ODD – SHERRIE WELLER

I was three when we picked up my little brother from the hospital. My sister, who looked like me in every way except for a small mole in the middle of my right cheek, stood next to me. I remember hanging over the seemingly huge front seat of the white wood paneled Squire station wagon staring at the tiny bundle with tufts of black hair sticking straight up out of the soft white cotton blanket with yellow and blue stripes held in my mother's arms. I remember the howling wind blowing snow across the highway, Dad trying desperately to get my sister and me to sit down and put our seatbelts on, but there was no tearing us away from our firm stance. Chins resting on the brown vinyl, reaching over to touch the ebony fuzz on this new creature's head, full of questions about this strange little person that we had picked up like a watermelon at the grocery store. Why is he so pink? Why can't I touch his nose and his fingers? Why is he crying? It did not seem odd to me then, picking up a baby from the hospital. It did not seem odd that my mother's stomach had never grown large or that she had not been in the hospital as well. I was three. I had heard the word adoption many times before. It did not seem odd at all.

    My sister tells me that when she was little, she thought that our parents found our brother in a drawer. Not through adoption, nor through Catholic Social Services at St. Mary's Hospital, but a drawer. I press her on this memory, ask, "What do you mean? Did you think they just opened a random drawer somewhere and there he was?" She bristles. I want her to be able to describe what she thought when she was three years old. She says she can't, all she can access is the vague outline about the drawer. I tell her I have a vivid memory of going to pick him up from the hospital. Knowing he was adopted, just like us. I am curious about the discrepancy between our remembered experience. Our conversation ends, but the drawer image lingers. I can't dislodge it from my head and I start to fill it in: A couple is led into a room where the walls are covered with drawers, small drawers, drawers the size of a sock drawer. Gurgling sounds and small sighs escape from all around them. A somber-faced nun, clad in a full habit draped over a plump, meat and potatoes body, brings them to the wall directly across from the door. She turns, twitches a slightly benevolent smile and pulls open a drawer. There, in a down-lined interior, lies a newborn, sleeping peacefully. His thick black hair sticks out defiantly around his face. The nun reaches in with crinkled, age-spotted hands and picks up the dozing child without disturbing his slumber. She gently places him into the waiting arms of the woman, pauses and nods. The nun leans over, kisses the gift-laden lady on the cheek, shakes the man's hand. Without words, she leads them out. Tinkling silver lullaby music drifts into the hallway. The vision is fuzzy, everything soft and blurred. The drawers are silent.

THE LANGUAGE OF FLOWERS – BIBI WEIN

"This is called Queen Anne's Lace."

My father doesn't remember telling me this as we walked in a meadow on a summer morning when I was 5 or 6, but it's one of the most important things he ever said to me. It was a rare pleasure—both to be in the country, and to be with him. More than half a century later, he remains a preferred companion of small children. He addresses them with a gravitas and clarity that lends the listener some of the importance with which his lilting baritone imbues the fact at hand: "This is called Queen Anne's Lace."

I was an attentive child, and especially attentive to my father, whose voice and tone could elevate the plainest statement to the realm of potent secrets. The little girl I was looked at the foam of white flowers afloat on the meadow and saw something intricate, fragile, and mysterious. And that is the way I see this flower still. Never mind that all my field guides tell me it's a "noxious weed."

The creamy blossom is actually a compound inflorescence made up of many florets, each no bigger than an embroidery stitch, grouped together in a broad, flat cluster called an umbel. In the center, sometimes, and only sometimes, is a purple stitch--a single dark floret, almost hidden among the white. This purple floret doesn't produce seeds like the others. Its function? No one knows.

When he took me walking on that long-ago summer morning, my father had been speaking English for only a few years, and though he might have seen Queen Anne's Lace in his native Europe, he surely learned its name from my American-born mother. Language fascinated both my parents, and I'm sure it was the blossom's *name* that appealed to them: the nuance of royalty and its suggestion of dignity and value in a flower growing wild.

My mother played the piano, and wrote poetry and songs. She also painted, and she attached great weight to the names of colors. Long before kindergarten, I could identify Crayola's 48—chartreuse, indigo, violet, magenta—and much of what was in my mother's paintbox of oils as well:

carnelian, burnt sienna, raw umber, cadmium yellow, cobalt, cerulean. But not all intriguing words came from crayons or tubes of paint. Some belonged to flowers. Lady's Slipper was one my mother liked for its descriptive whimsy, Black-eyed Susan for its personification, larkspur for its sound, the same for periwinkle—not merely a flower, but also a color—which she used in a poem to paint the sky.

Passion and intensity were qualities my parents shared. Their mutual devotion was never in doubt, and their feeling for each other carried over into everything that interested them, large and small. Their enthusiasms were lifelong, never transitory. But what they didn't understand or care about—for example, anything that smacked of science or numbers, and all physical activity that demanded more skill than a brisk walk—was disdained and dismissed.

The other children in our West Philadelphia neighborhood were taught to swim, roller skate, jump rope, and ride bikes, but all I was permitted was hopscotch. My parents didn't know how to do any of these things and they believed I'd be safer if *I* didn't do them. But what they did teach me was music. Also words. Contemporary neuroscientists who study music and the brain would find a link between the music that filled the rooms of my earliest years and the eagerness with which my young mind stored up words and soon began putting them together.

Thanks to my father's origins in a fractured Eastern Europe, my mother's crisp memory for her high school French and Latin, *her* mother's Russian lullabies, and the mellifluous Italian my parents' friends sang on Saturday nights around our upright piano, the flavors of eight languages apart from English informed my sound world. And then there was the language of the garden. An imaginary garden until I was well into adulthood. Though my parents routinely provided me with definitions, the larkspur and periwinkle and lady's slipper were all just "flowers." Though their names fixed themselves in my mind like the Russian lyrics of my grandmother's lullabies, which I can't translate but can still repeat today, *larkspur* and *periwinkle* were as abstract as random words in an unfamiliar tongue. But Queen Anne's Lace—that I had *seen*, and would instantly recognize throughout my life in a meadow full of strangers.

Ubiquitous as this wildflower is, it hasn't taken hold in the cold north woods where I now have a cabin, and I've failed, so far, to transplant or seed it in my garden. So at least once each summer, I make a pilgrimage of some 30 miles to cut a dozen stalks for a bouquet. I know a lonely road where dazzles of cardinal flowers hide among pink Joe-Pye weed and spunky Black-eyed Susan in a beaver meadow by a rocky stream. Most spectacular of all, towering above rosy steeplebush, great bristly burdock and the golden-eyed blooms of pearly everlasting, are certain giants. They are the ultimate of their species, a thousand tiny petals on each frothy umbel, some swelling in a spiral around that tiny purple mystery, others arranged in concentric circles of exquisite symmetry. The huge blossoms are as varied and ethereal as snowflakes. Their filagreed leaves arch over the roadside on sensuous, branching stems six and seven feet tall. This is called Queen Anne's Lace.

OVERLOOKING THE BLUE RIDGE PARKWAY – TAMMY TILLOTSON

Before turning me a loose
my father said, "Child,
you need to learn to be still."
He didn't understand my rush –
we were all going to the same place,
we were all gonna get there eventually.
I had to see the mountain range
up close, personally needed
to be there first.
I stepped fearlessly onto the ledge,
arms spread like the morning fog
believing here was happy dying.
Seeped in heavenly haze,
at first I didn't notice
the man knelt beside the wall.
His fog-colored suit
matched tufts of fog-colored hair.
He used a cane to right himself,
and lifting his eyes,
he flashed a sickening grin.
I listened carefully,
for distant footsteps
I listened
but heard not one.
His gaze burned,
"Child, do you know Jesus?
Have you been saved?"
My heart heard
the calmest whisper
Nod, and you'll be safe.
He patted my head,
said more to himself than to me,
"You're such a good little girl,"
smiling as he left.
While my father read his suspicious tract,
I stood very still.

MY MAMA CHEATING ON MY DADDY WITH JAMES BROWN – KELI STEWART

i ain't playing. ever since i was me,
they be in the kitchen making music with dish-soap.

she wear hot pants, mumbling over grits,
smacking baby roaches flat against walls, bringing fingers down in a snap.

she be snaking, grinding over grease spots.
they keep door closed. i can't see, but i hear.

he be talking 'bout please, please
please, please, please,
please   she say   *give it to me james*   *do it james*   *sing it james*

after a while smells come from the kitchen. they sex smoke smell like steak.
         washing powder. on thursdays, always chicken. other times, like tears.

james brown be with her over the sink where sometime she just stare at
         dishwater.   my daddy work nights, sleep days.

that's how james brown started giving her something good. she say they be
doing something mu   sical, not sex   ual.

i don't know how she do it. cook and cheat at the same time. wash and
         cheat.
iron and cheat. fold and cheat. mop and cheat. sing and cheat.

i don't know how she do it. housewife at 25. one child, three children
dead, manage two men.

THE BB GUN – D. L. HALL

In the earliest pool party photograph, I am a year old, squatting in a light blue dress next to the vinyl, blow-up pool and splashing a tiny hand in the water. My mother wears a white, sleeveless turtleneck shirt and hand-made, navy pedal-pushers. Her lipstick is shocking red against pale skin, and the top lids of her green eyes are painted with a thin stroke of dark eyeliner. Her face is full of light and youth. She is nineteen years old when I'm turning one in 1964.

Over the years, the pools get bigger and by the time I'm eight, it's a thin metal circle about three feet tall. My friends and I drag metal foldout chairs to the rim, so we can jump in. The neighborhood gang is here: Gene, Jesus, and Steve. We carry on the same arguments as the previous day. I've been feeling combative lately, and there is a tension growing in me that I don't understand, but this week, I've focused all my energy on fighting my parents for the gift I want this year, a gift I can't do without: a BB gun.

My younger cousins are present and my aunt Nelda is here. Because she is only four years older than I, we get along fine. When Nelda bosses me, I obey. It seems a natural order. She is not a contentious playmate; in fact, I admire her, finding myself interested in anything in which she's interested. So I don't try to show *her* whose party it is, but Steve, Jesus and Gene are another story. I intend to make them as miserable in my pool as Steve has made me in his. In fact, I'm tired of the way the boys make up rules to benefit themselves when we play cops and robbers or when we swim in Steve's pool—which is a larger, more permanent, above-the-ground pool. So, I am preoccupied, today, with clarifying the rules because lately, nothing seems fair. The politics of pool play depend on several factors, the most important being whose yard the pool is in. Today, we're in *my* yard, it's *my* pool, and *my* birthday.

In the water, the energy is spiraling. We're climbing on the chairs to jump into the water, and I'm trying to tell the boys that I don't want my face wet and let's all jump in together. From a chair, Steve pauses before jumping and

I say, "Let's all count to three." But while I'm counting, Steve jumps in and Jesus follows yelling, "Geronimo!" and Gene says "three" before I've said "two" and so I follow Gene, but when we come up from the water, I'm mad and remind the unruly boys that it is my yard. It is enough that I'm nervous my parents won't get me the BB gun for which I've begged stubbornly over the course of the last week, but my friends have shirked my authority on my day when my stomach is already in knots.

This bossiness feels like a tornado inside me. The boys are beginning to leave me out of their play because I win when we argue, but lose the races. I'm confused about how their bodies are getting faster and stronger than mine. Their interests are beginning to change. Just a few days ago, I found them in the field by Gene's house huddled in the cardboard box in which his mama's new washing machine arrived. Across the entrance they had scribbled "Boys Club. No Girls" in black marker. "No Girls" referred only to me. I stood outside the box trying to convince them that this would never work. No reasoning would bring them out. When Gene said, "Go away," I kicked the side, and I heard the squeal of laughter. I stood a moment, thinking, then I stomped home, returned with my baseball bat, and began pummeling the walls. Each hit barely dented the side, but it made a loud whap and boys scampered out like roaches. When they were outside, they stood watching, disbelieving that I'd do something like this. "Alright, alright," Steve said, trying to stop me. "You can join the club, but you got to pay ten cents." I looked at him hard, my chest heaving. I swung the bat again and marched home.

It's been a few days since I wrecked their club, so when Steve splashes me in my eyes in my pool because he's hyper and enjoying himself, I wallop him across the face because I'm still mad about the club trick not to mention that I clearly said *I don't want my face wet*. While he's crying into his mother's apron, Aunt Nelda poses for the camera in front of him in her flowered one piece with an exaggerated smile that makes her eyes squint shut and for the remainder of my days, I have evidence of my early temper and urge to rule others.

After the cake and homemade vanilla ice cream, it's time to open the presents. I am anxious to get to the present from my parents. I have insisted that I must have a BB gun. The thing is, Steve has BB gun, and he won't let me play with it when I want. He lets Jesus shoot it, but tells me I have to wait my turn, and he checks with Gene before he finally lets me have a turn. So I am dying for my own BB gun, but my mother is against the idea. She says again and again that under no circumstance is she willing to get me a gun, and if I don't change my mind, I'll get body powder and bath bubbles. My father is also against the idea but for a different reason. He says I'll get tired of it, and it'll sit in a corner. He says, "It's a phase," but I know he's a gun-loving man, and I'm gambling that somehow he'll change his mind and talk sense into my mother.

Standing against my parents has required great strength, and I have this woozy feeling that, in the end, they'll admire my tenacity, as well as purchase the gun for me. I have separated the reality of my mother's objections from a magic world of possibilities that I've created and believe in. It feels like a risk worth taking, and so, on purpose, I haven't prepared for any conclusion except *getting the gun*. Otherwise, I could jinx the whole thing.

When my mom announces that it's time to open the presents, I begin tearing off wrapping paper of presents from my aunts and uncles, quickly saying thank-you's and opening the next, while friends from the street stand nearby eating ice cream. My guests, I presume, have no idea what's at stake, and my own curiosity feels like a bubble ready to burst. After each present my mother tells me to hold it up and smile. She clicks the camera.

I am in the center of a circle of paper when I get to the last present. It is a Ken doll my Aunt Gloria has given me, and I tell Jesus, "Now you don't have to be Barbie next time we play," and I show him the doll. Gene snickers, but I don't know why, he still has to be Barbie. Steve laughs because he always gets to be Ken with my old, beat-up doll and says Jesus makes a good Barbie. Everyone laughs.

I lean over and search through the disheveled paper. There are no more presents. Confused, I look up and see my mother holding a small, square box wrapped in pink paper. She is smiling as she hands the box to me. I read her face and see something like victory in her eyes. She seems so pleased with herself that I'm taken aback. I swallow a gulp of air. When I accept the box from her hands, I have to look away from her eyes. I stare at this box. Alarms sound inside of me. My insides roil. I am so unprepared for this outcome that I lower my head. I'm afraid I'm going to cry. I let my long hair hang into my face as I turn the present over in my hands, not opening it, trying to understand what this means about the world. The realization that she has won hits me, and I understand that she is enjoying this, which complicates my disappointment. It seems like I have learned that if one sticks to a decision, if one really believes, things work out. Somewhere I got the idea that tenacity is rewarded, but it feels like a murky, dreamlike memory. This is not about a BB gun; but I can't name it. It feels larger than me, larger than my house, or the town I live in. It feels deep like a slumbering darkness when I close my eyes, like being left at the mall or alone in the dark in the big-girl bedroom.

As I untangle tape slowly from the box, my tears begin to hit the paper. I can't stop them, and this humiliation is especially cruel as the boys who will not let me boss them stand watching. I start talking to my feelings, asking the tears to stop, panicking at the thought of everyone witnessing this crushing blow, and realizing how unprepared I am. *It's body powder. It's body powder. I can't believe it.* I wonder how I'll ever look into my mother's face again, and I cannot look up from this box. I tear at the paper slowly, deliberately, trying hard not to lose control.

When I drop the last piece of wrapping, I wipe my eye with the back of one hand, and Aunt Kay notices. She stops laughing and looks concerned. I can hardly get the box open. My chest is heaving. What I really want to do is to drop it all and run into the cane fields behind the house and spend the rest of my life punishing my parents with my absence. Aunt Kay reaches forward and helps me lift the box top from the bottom. I blink, clearing the tears. I wipe the other eye. It takes a moment to recognize what I see and when I do, I'm bewildered, and I blink again, harder. The contents are blurry, but as I blink I see yellow tubes. It already feels like I've gone to hell, and this is too shocking. The box is full of cardboard tubes of BBs. I look up, stunned, forgetting to hide my tears. The crowd clearly sees my red, wet face, and their smiles drop as they realize something is happening that they don't understand.

From the sewing room, my dad steps into the hallway. Behind him, the bathroom door is open and the bright July sun makes it impossible to see him clearly. We all see a man's form carrying a long, wrapped present. The wind sweeps into my lungs like a punch and I cry out, turning my devastation into glee as quick as a dive into the pool from a flimsy chair. Wiping strands of damp hair, I open the present with gusto to reveal a brown, shiny Daisy BB gun. I jump up and hug each parent. It feels as if I've been grabbed in mid-air and saved from stepping off a cliff by a large hand at the nape of my neck. They both seem a little surprised that I am this excited over a BB Gun.   I do not own the words to explain or defend myself and so, I try to forget about the whole thing, but it is not lost on me that sometime before that pool party, my father went to Hendrix Hardware and handed over his sugar mill money to Mr. Hendrix for a BB gun for his daughter, so she could walk among the boys, loaded.

ROMANCE – BEATRICE M. HOGG

Romaine liked everyone to call her "Romance," and to me, a nine-year-old in the mid-sixties, Romance is what she represented. She looked good, she smelled good, and no man could resist her. When she came to visit my parents, even the air was charged with sensuality. I watched her in awe and admiration.

A fine brown woman, with her hair carefully pressed and waved, Romance's makeup was perfect too, and she carried lipstick and a compact in order to keep it looking just right. Like many colored women of that time, she wore a tight girdle under tight dresses. She had beautiful legs, and wore open-toed shoes. Her ample bosom and wide hips, accentuated a walk that drew you in like a smoldering blues. The scent of perfume and powder trailed behind her. She could play the piano and sing the blues in a wicked, sultry voice. She smoked her cigarettes with a gold holder. Even before I knew what sexy was, I knew that Miss Romance was "IT."

I was always excited when I saw Romaine's car pull up in front of our house. An aura of mystery surrounded her. I never knew her age, but I guessed her to be fortyish or fiftyish, years younger than my adopted parents. Whenever she came to visit, my parents usually sent me to my room. I could tell Romaine was downstairs telling dirty jokes, because the grownups whispered then exploded into waves of laughter. Sometimes, when she played my piano, I was allowed to listen, but I couldn't decipher the lyrical codes that made the women blush and men shake their heads. Certain words would trigger laughter and smiles, while I looked on incredulously. Usually, I returned to my room not understanding the stories that had been told with a sigh and a wink. When we went to the local beer tavern in our coal-mining town, Romaine would entice all of the men, black and white. Men liked Romance.

Once, she gave me a black and white portrait of herself, a picture that was even prettier than my black and white postcard of Miss Dinah Washington. Miss Romance was so beautiful, I wanted to be just like her. I couldn't imagine what it would be like to be as worldly and seductive as Romaine. Her smile held secrets, secrets that I would never know.

I don't know what ever happened to Romaine over the years. It seemed she just stopped coming around as my parents got older and sicker. I'm sure she is long gone by now, but I'll never forget her and what she meant to me when I was a shy, awkward little girl.

Forty years later, I still see snatches of Romaine's style and spirit in other black women. In "The Color Purple," Shug Avery had that Romaine thing going on. I still dream of being like Miss Romaine, being a confident, sexy black woman who can turn a few heads. Alas, I don't have the figure, nor the walk, but sometimes when I dress up for a special night, I channel her spirit. I think of her fragrance when I rub scented lotion into my skin until it gleams and I comb my hair until it is just right. On the rare occasions when I wear makeup, I remember her rouged cheeks and lips as I apply blush and bright red lipstick. When I put on long earrings that tinkle when I move my neck, an armful of bangles that clang when I shake my hand, and a necklace that shows off my bosom, I know Miss Romaine would be proud.

Just once, I would like to create the sensation that Romaine did. Just once, I would like to be the feast, the delicacy that no man can resist. Just once, I would like to cause the heads to turn, to see men licking their lips and wiping their brows in the wake of my strut. Just one chance to be the embodiment of a dream. I believe there is a little Romance every brown-skinned colored gal, just waiting to be let out. Now that I am fiftyish, too, armed with a heart full of secrets and able to sing my own blues, that time has finally arrived. It's time for Romance.

AT THE EMBERS – ANDREA POTOS

Two sisters, nine and ten, sit with their father
in the foyer of the restaurant.
It is a Tuesday in September, a day
for surprises he told them when he picked
them up at school and drove them
to Embers in the High Ridge Mall.

It isn't often I lunch with my girls, is it
he asks and they blush, his arms
cupping their shoulders as they wait
for someone he works with, his
secretary, to arrive. She's been there
for me when I needed her he tells them,

and he wants to include her, and they will
all keep this their secret he says. She arrives,
a chestnut-haired woman with smiles,
and they file into a corner booth
where the restaurant lamps seem too dim for
daylight, and the leather seats red as deep

as their mother's lipstick, red as deep
as the day the youngest fell off her bike
and sliced her knee, the blood
staining her white kneesocks minutes after Dad
removed the training wheels and promised her that
everything, absolutely everything,
would be okay.

ANNMARIE'S BEAR – LOUISE SCHNURR

Dec 14, 1996

Dear Eva,

If you were to open this box without reading this explanation, you would be puzzled as to why Grammie would send you a straggly, bear for a Christmas present. But this is a very special bear for a very special granddaughter! Annmarie slept with this bear every night from the time she was a tiny baby until she died at ten. She loved it! It was given to her by her big brother, Dan, for either her first birthday or her first Christmas.

Much love,
XXXXOOOOO
Grammie

This is my response to my grandmother's letter:

Sometimes at night a bear pads around in my things. Because he is sleepy and grouchy, he is dangerous. He breathes so deeply that he vacuums the air in my room. Because you cannot out run a bear, I lie prone, play dead. He pulls at the cave of my blankets looking for something, someone.

One evening I leave strawberry jam on the stairs hoping to calm him, but still I hear him creak up to my loft. Lost in a trance, he is grieving and I am afraid. I try calling out some bear names, hoping to still his rage. "Pooh, Paddington, dress bear." He doesn't respond.

He has been around for thousands of years. He has eaten from my grandmother's blackberry bushes. Once he mauled her furnace. She forgot his magic, left him alone in her daughter's bed. She picked a coffin lined with pink satin to match the inside of his ears, but she left him on a shelf. Morning after morning he looked at the perfectly smooth sheets where the ten-year-old should have been. He slept night after night alone. He made demands that a child could no longer answer. He combed his fur with a brush full of child hair.

Now he lies down with me, hoping to wake from a bad dream. He howls but the dark muffles his rage. I reach to protect him with my arms. He nuzzles my heart to reveal his pain. "Children die easily," he whispers to the night.

When the grandmother boxed him up, she promised him a picnic with ants in Amherst. He plans it every night. He puts in the basket a cloth, a bottle of ginger ale, a box of animal crackers. He expects my aunt to be there at a teddy bear's picnic, untouched by time.

My eighty-year-old grandmother believes I can tame him. She expects me to trap him in my ancestor worship. Instead, I beg him to tell me the stories of my father who bought him with a newspaper boy's tips. He remembers only an appointment with death.

I try to remember Annmarie's face, how to tame his heart. One morning I bring him to a breakfast of cinnamon honey and toast. He sits on my mother's oak chair calmed by the smells of my 10-year-old body.

That night he leads me in the starry dark to a honey tree where I find my aunt at last, holding her breath, waiting. He clambers up the tree, brings us bees and honey to eat. We three hold each other calling to my grandmother about grief.

ABOVE THE HARD EARTH – SUSAN LEAHY

Loud man-voices threaten. Words, curses blur. I am in darkness and afraid of what is going on. My brother asks if I'm awake and do I hear it. "Yeah, what should we do?" I ask. "I don't know," he answers, "It just started." We lie in the dark, he in his twin bed and I in the lower bunk. The angry voices escalate: Dad and John. Mom is trying to calm them down, intervene. But she's angry, too. Things slam and crash; maybe doors, maybe one of them. My brother and I decide to creep downstairs to see. John is leaning against a wall, half keeled over. He doesn't look good. He's drunk and Dad's really mad. John's tattooed friend is by the front door, drunk. We go back upstairs and wonder how we'll go to school the next day with no sleep. The voices continue for a while and then quiet down. Mom and Dad stay up talking, fuming. Finally, silence.

The phone rings on a Saturday night. The Miss America Pageant is on and it is all very fancy. They are about to announce the winner; it is almost eleven. My brother answers the phone and puts Mom on. She looks serious, then alarmed and then frightened. She thanks them for calling and walks quickly up to her room to wake up Daddy. "John's been shot." He bolts out of bed and grabs his clothes. Their look goes from shock to resignation. They are really not surprised. It's something almost expected. They dress and take a cab to the hospital. My brother is in charge of us and we don't know when they'll get home. On Monday morning, back in third grade, I'm the kid with the story to tell. "My brother was shot. He got sixteen holes in his intestines." "With a gun?" my friends ask. "Didn't he die?" My parents come home from the hospital and rage about his anger, his throwing things at them in the room. He returns home a week later, carrying a dungaree jacket with the coolest hole at the waistband. I put my finger through the ragged circle and imagine a bullet searing through, the bullet that remains lodged in his hipbone. Whenever my mother turns her back, John laughs, raising his shirt to show me his raw, pink scar that makes me nauseous. I scream.

After years of tension, a pattern emerges. Every three weeks, something pops; an arrest, a fight, detox or jail. The sanctuary of calm and safety is always broken. I visit John in rehab in Hell's Kitchen when I'm eleven. He gets into a fight with a counselor behind closed doors; I hear a chair hit the wall. I visit him in Riker's Island when I'm twelve, where the guards are mean to me. We visit him in rehab again, upstate this time, when I'm thirteen. I write to him in jail during my freshman year. I tell him about the boys I like. He writes constantly, long letters filled with advice about being good for Mom and Dad, growing up and boys. We don't go to the therapy that Mom and Dad go to. Protected from that, we are protected from helping him and left to agonize through it on our own.

It is dinnertime. Mom and I are in the kitchen cooking. Dad comes downstairs after changing, flipping on the living room lights. He screams, "He's blue." John lies on the couch, his face and lips matching the royal blue of the industrial-strength couch Mom bought years before. He is making sounds and I stuff my hand in his mouth to look for the thing he wears on his rotten front tooth. He must be choking on it. I can't find it. I dial 911 and my mother stares at me, grateful and surprised. John's arms and legs move, like a convulsion. The ambulance drivers tell us he will be okay. My parents follow him to the hospital. Mom turns to us and says, "Take the lasagna out when it's done." As if we will eat dinner while our brother dies on the way. I grab my jacket and go with my parents, who are refused by John into the recovery room. He allows me in, a safer and less confrontational bet, following this overdose. He's awake. It's surreal; I already saw him dead. Yet here he is, still a bit blue, flirting with the nurse who rolls her eyes. "You almost died," I tell him. "Your palms are blue." He looks at his upturned hand, confused.

A year later, the ground frozen, his coffin is supported above a crater. No one is surprised. We are in pain and yet freer, safer than ever before. I expect to stay there until they put him in the ground, but my other brother tugs my shoulder and says, "It's time to go." I hate leaving John there, above the hard earth. Months later, in the chill air, some of the flowers still seem fresh.

BLACK CAT – MARJORIE MANWARING

Fourth grade, last-minute Halloween costume—
construction paper eye mask, ears on a headband.

Black bodysuit clings to unwelcome breast beginnings
grabbed like handfuls of candy corn

by an orange-haired clown who giggles, scampers off.
I wish the mask concealed my hot red cheeks

flee to my desk, put on a winter coat
busy myself making tissue-paper ghosts.

ROSES – EMILY LEVINE

Jacob was missing from his usual chair that day. It was a rainy, typically dull day in fifth grade math class, the kind of day during which you would rather be anywhere else- except for where Jacob was. I remember when our math class got the call, but I also remember that we were not told right away what had happened.

Jacob was shy and quirky. He was the kind of kid who was neither popular nor pariah; he was not sugary sweet or outrageously opinionated. He was part of the "Blockheads" club, a special math club for the most brilliant math students in the fifth grade, and he loved to build elaborate forts on the sprawling thirty-three acres of nature that was our elementary school, Nueva. But most of all, Jacob had an obsessive, intense, but unrequited crush on a girl in our grade, and that girl was me.

A couple hours after math class, the entire fifth grade was rounded up and told that something serious had happened, and Jacob would not be returning to school for a while. We were told that he was suffering from a large tumor in his brain, and that it was deadly and cancerous. He had woken up one night with a horrible headache that would not go away, and when his parents finally took him to the hospital, he was diagnosed with brain cancer. I remember not knowing what a tumor was, but I know that my mom nearly collapsed when I told her in the kitchen that day.

At the time, I did not realize how precious life was, in the same way I did not realize how precious I was to Jacob. He was so in love with me that for my birthday he bought me eighty dollars worth of beautiful red roses, so when he asked me to be his girlfriend at age ten I could not resist. His mom later told me that just the thought of me being his girlfriend helped him get through each day. Looking back on it, it amazes me that I could have provided someone with that much courage and power just by being.

As Jacob's cancer grew, he changed forever. His speech became slurred and impaired, and his messy, long hair that he had dyed bright blue before his diagnosis soon withered and fell out. At first, everyone at school visited him in the hospital and showered him with gifts, but over time, most people moved on with their lives. Unfortunately, Jacob could not move on with his. I continued to visit Jacob frequently, but sadly, I too lost touch with him after I moved to Palo Alto.

    A couple of years ago I went to Jacob's junior high graduation. After the ceremony ended, each of the graduates was given a rose. I ran into Jacob outside the gymnasium and greeted him with a huge smile and a warm hug. To my shock, he didn't know who I was because his memory had been permanently damaged. The other kids tried to jog his memory by saying my name over and over, but all Jacob could do was smile shyly at me and shake his head in confusion. He could barely speak, but when he stuttered that he thought I was beautiful and handed me his rose, my heart hurt with a bittersweet nostalgia. As he looked into my eyes quickly before turning around to walk over to his parents, I felt a familiar connection that comforted me. I'll never know what Jacob was thinking before he waved goodbye to me for the last time, but I continue to hope that for that one second, in a deep part of his memory, he remembered.

FLYING: ROUND AND ROUND – JENELLE TABOR

Recess! We jump from our desks and race to the coat wall. In a flurry of flopping sleeves and hoods we crowd the classroom door. Still scrambling with buttons and zippers we throw ourselves into the stream of fellow students pouring down the central hallway. The stream swells as each classroom empties. We are a tsunami of coat colors and textures with a single, jabbering, raucous voice. Jostling for position the colors weave in and around each other as we flow toward the double doors. Hands and forearms slap out to those doors and after a fractional moment the dam bursts. With a surge of glee we spread out into the bright playground.

It is an Indian summer morning, the best time of year in Seattle, still early enough for the air to feel fresh and cool, but late enough that the fog has burned off and taken with it, the earlier clammy chill. Having walked through that chill on the way to school this morning, I am glad the day is now warming up. I used to ride a school bus, snug in the humid surrounds of fogged windows, green vinyl seat benches, and kids revving up for the day, our happy chatter loud enough to override the noise of the bus' diesel engine. Then the school district built a new school, so much closer to my home. At the same time, they closed two older schools across the district. Rearranging the distribution of children amongst schools, they transferred all the kids in my neighborhood to the new school. Everyone that is, except me and my siblings.

My mom had a thing against making kids change schools. She didn't want her children forced to break from the place and people with which they felt secure. However, after a year of hustling seven kids through each weekday morning, then driving the youngest three to their old school, I'm sure she was relieved to realize that with the rest of the kids in the neighborhood transferred to the new school, we youngest would not be alone in a sea of unfamiliar faces.

The girls in my class race for the monkey bars. This set of monkey bars is different than the one at the old school. The old one was a simple thing that looked like two ladders connected at the top by a third horizontal ladder. This new one is much bigger. It is like a skyscraper under construction, a skeleton of steel five levels high. Round bars, cold enough to burn, sketch grid sections each two feet square. The bottom level of the structure is the widest and tallest. It is five grid sections across and three high. On each of its four sides, the middle grid sections are lacking their lowest bars. These are the entry ways and the hallways through the structure. The second level is three grid sections across and one high. The top level is a single cube.

The first four girls to reach the structure claim the "swinging bars," or what are the top of the four entry ways. As the rest of us climb over and through the structure, those first four wrap their coats around their chosen bars. Each then hooks a leg over the now insulated and cushioned bars. After hoisting themselves up to perch momentarily on the backs of the thighs of the hooked legs, and grabbing onto rungs around their heads, they jiggle about to find just the right spot on the backs of those thighs from which to launch. Then, with a quick breath and a duck they grab their hooked legs' ankles and fling themselves over and around their bars, becoming wheels, spinning around their bar axles.

I never could get the hang of swinging. It didn't look all that hard, but it always hurts the back of my leg, regardless of how I wrapped my coat, or what spot on my thigh I chose from which to launch myself. I tried repeatedly to get it right, with girls calling out instructions and tips, but finally, I had to give it up. I guessed I just wasn't tough enough or limber enough, or something. Each time I failed I felt more uncoordinated, more cloddish.

Climbing to the top of the highest level where a breeze cools my scalp, I can see the whole playground. Kids are everywhere, playing kickball, tether ball and hopscotch, lined up for turns on the swings and the slide. Squeals of delight come from those clinging to the whirling merry-go-round. Other kids just race around each other, hollering, enrapt in games of their own making. Below me, girls are switching out turns on the swinging bars. Soon, one of them will urge me to try, again, to learn how to do it right. I can see the exhilaration in their eyes. How they sparkle beforehand, with anticipation. How they sparkle afterward with the thrill of speed. Like swinging on a swing set, swinging on the bars is like flying, but on the bars you can fly faster. The world zooms by in a blur. So, I understand why they enjoy it so much, why they want to share that thrill with me, but that is never going to happen.

Aside from the pain, I have another difficulty with the swinging bars. It's the same difficulty I have with the merry-go-round. Motion sickness. At one time, I had thought that by forcing myself to get on the merry-go-round, time and again, I would eventually inure myself to the dizziness and blooming nausea. No such luck. Just thinking about it makes my stomach threaten. Maybe this is what really keeps me from being able to "swing." I can't let myself be free enough to really let go. I'm simply too afraid I will get sick all over myself, or worse, someone else. Then the sparkle in their eyes will turn to disgust. I had already experienced their pitying looks, after my previous, failed attempts. I had weathered those looks by laughing off my failures and making jokes about double-jointed knees and super-sensitive legs, but you can't just laugh off vomit.

My third and final difficulty with the swinging bars is not the bars at all, but the girls swinging on them. Of this group of girls, thrown together after the redistribution of kids in the district, there are only a few of whom I know well. Even after two years at this school, I am still defining my place in this group, this group who had an extra year to develop swinging skills, this group who isn't worried about nausea, and worst of all, this group who is "girlish."

These girls wear dresses all the time, new, in style, store-bought dresses. Not old hand-me-downs or plain, easy to sew, boxy dresses. These girls wear tights, not socks that fall down without rubber bands to hold them up. These girls have their hair done up fancy by their mothers. My mom feels lucky if she can get us all out of the house on time and fully clothed. No, disgorging my breakfast would not go well with these girlish girls.

I need to stop the invitations to swing. I want my place in this group to be defined by some ability uniquely mine, not by pity for my failure at swinging, and certainly not by disgust because I got sick on someone's shiny shoes. I need to come up with something I can do, something just as good as swinging.

From my monkey bar aerie, I take another look at all the kids on the playground and what they are doing. I don't run fast; can't kick a ball hard or far enough. I can do hopscotch, but so can most everyone. Well, who can't slide down a slide or swing on a swing? Let's just skip over the merry-go-round. Tether ball? That would hurt if you got smacked upside the head with that thing. Besides, it goes round and round. Moving on...

A discussion below distracts my thoughts. "My dad says it's disgusting, that they were right to ban it. He said he wouldn't want us kids to see it."

"See what?" I ask, my interest piqued at what parents don't want kids to see.

"Naked people in paintings and sculpture," said one of the girls.

"But, that's art. It's not like it's pornography. It's different if it's art," I say, loftily.

"My dad doesn't think kids should be exposed to nudity," said the first girl. "He said it leads to curiosity in all the wrong things."

"Some of the most famous artwork in the world has naked people in it. Are we supposed to just throw away all that old art?" In a pompous voice I mimic an imaginary, self-righteous bureaucrat. "Forget about what we've valued for centuries. We can't let children see naked body parts. Good God! They'll ask what they're for!" In my own voice I add, "Besides, it's just the human body. We are beautiful. We should appreciate our bodies, not act like there's something dirty about them."

And the debate is on. Never mind that we are just 10 year-olds, spouting what we have heard adults say. My scan of the playground activities is forgotten. This is fun. I like a good debate. My mind flits between possible responses to points made. It's not just what you say, but how you say it. I keep a running track of the numbers for and against as minds change and new thoughts occur. In my aerie, I feel like a conductor directing the play of an orchestra. Excited, I stand up inside the top cube. My body stretches out over the top bar, the better to see all the girls below me. Unrestrained, my arms gesticulate compellingly as I make another point, when I realize… this is it. I can talk. I can argue. I can change minds. Another breeze lifts my hair, and it occurs to me that there are different kinds of flying. Going round and round bodily may make me retch, but I can happily go round and round with words all day long.

PIVOT – LITA KURTH

Pivot: a pin serving for attachment

At noon, my father unhitches the workhorse from the load of logs. In winter coats, we sit on a sunny boulder, open his lunchbox shaped like a rural mailbox, and eat fat slices of homemade bread and cheese wrapped in waxed paper. Coffee steams from the thermos. In the snowy shade of an evergreen, he shows us round red berries, white inside: wintergreen. He gives them all to us; after, we chew the shiny fresh leaves. Almost candy. Crows cry in the blue sky, settle high in pines.

With his axe he cuts a notch on the tree's far side and points: "Stand back there, and don't move." The Homelite chainsaw putters, roars to life, and complains its way through the thick trunk. The treetop wobbles, tentative, then tips, soft, then hurried, rushing, breaking the *popple* branches, and *Wham*! The ground reverberates beneath our soles. With excited cries, we run to bounce on the fallen branches. He saws the big tree into logs.

The last cord is stacked, and cold pinches our toes. He sets us high on old Pat's back, behind the two brass harness nobs. We are queens carried by warm muscles. Clop, clop, the tufted hooves rise and fall.

"Somebody take off my boots," he says in his scratchy voice. I untie the sawdusty knot, unloop the leather shoelace from hooks, loosen the crisscrosses near the toes, then pull with all my might, falling back with an empty boot in my hands. After bean soup, pickles, and bread, he lies on the floor. Giggling, we walk across his back. One by one, we ease his muscles.

Pivot: that on which something turns, hinges, or depends

My father sees me reading *Tales From the Red Fairy Book*. My father sees me reading *Tales From the Blue Fairy Book*. My father sees me reading *Tales From the Green Fairy Book*. "Why don't you cut out that god *damn* make-believe?"

At the big public library in town, he checks out a biography of Amelia Earhart and says, "Read this." I do, and I like it. But not as much as fairy tales. He checks out a book of travels in Tibet by Sven Hedin. "Read this." I do, and I like it. But not as much as fairy tales.

The morning of my patrol trip, a blue Wisconsin June, my father drives me to school. The gas is on E, but we make it.

I'm in the front seat coming home from a friend's; he's sweaty from work, his arm out the window, brown as a filbert. "Let's see how fast she'll go," he says. For just a minute, the needle leaps to 100 miles an hour, and the engine drowns out the radio. We swoop down the blacktop road, fields of oats and hay a blur. "I shouldn't do that," he apologizes, slowing with a smile.

Pivot: the person upon whom a line, as of troops, wheels about

Sticks stand in the ground with string pulled tight between them. A straight row of peas, of corn, a row of lettuce we'll eat with my mother's dressing: vinegar, sugar, and milk. A hill of potatoes, a hill of squash. Every seed comes up. We water through a coffee-can with nail-holes in the bottom. Ordered to, we carry buckets of gray and soapy water from the ringer washer in the cellar up to the garden.

"Get out there and pick some weeds." A curse. Burdock is the worst with roots like concrete pilings. "Ouch!" We step on thistles and whisper that we're slaves on dad's plantation.

One year he lets me have my own patch of gourds, green-striped like garter snakes, yellow and lumpy like scarred skin. I sell them to the neighbor for twenty-five cents a piece and buy pastel underpants embroidered with the days of the week.

He listens to *The Beer Barrel Polka*, "Pigs are Profitable," and the Grand Ole Oprey. When he's not around, we turn the dial to WIFC's top forty countdown.

Pivot: a pin or short shaft on the end of which something rests and turns, upon or about which something rotates or oscillates

My childhood rosary: The Depression ended with our first check from the WPA. "My friends. And you *are* my friends": FDR's voice on the radio, the Martin Luther King of the 1930's.

In the Marines, boys grew an inch or two when they finally had enough to eat. Chiang Kai-Shek was a baby butcher. Children starved in the streets while his warlords argued over who would sell the world's donations: food rotting in warehouses in the same city where orphans slept in horse-manure piles and froze to death.

My father sits in the green wooden rocker and sings. "Do you remember sweet Allie? She's sleeping in the valley. And the mockin'bird is singin' o'er her grave." "Farther along, we'll know all about it. Farther along, we'll understand why."

The corn and moon are high, and he says, "Let's take a walk. " We follow the rows, smelling green; the lightning bugs rise. "She was seven months pregnant, and he was gone. I came home on furlough and married Mum." I am silent with wonder. My older sister is my half sister.

My father lives in a room with a bookshelf made from boards and empty plastic kitty litter buckets. On a card table stand five different versions of the Bible: *King James, Good News for Modern Man, Revised Standard*, and others. *Luke* is the most beautiful Gospel. Portents and prophecies, destiny and dreams. "Don't kid yourself." Every event has a meaning; every life, a soul.

He boils brown rice with applesauce and honey, walks five miles a day, eats dates and calls them figs. He remembers when fields were full of prairie chickens, orioles, and cowbirds who laid their eggs in other birds' nests because they had to keep moving, to follow the cattle and their swarms of flies.

NUMBER ONE – ADRIAN GIBBONS KOESTERS

My younger sister Cece and I stood at the back door of my grandmother's house, watching a thunderstorm come down over the row houses and electric wires and thin wire fences that made up the nether landscape of our street. I was ten or eleven, I think; she would have been seven or eight. It was early summer, the thunder shower had just cracked, and we raced to the back door to get as close to the downpour as we could without being soaked. Some neighborhood kid had told me a thing earlier that was too good under the circumstances to keep to myself, so I leaned over and whispered to Cece, "*When it rains, God pees!*"

She giggled back as dangerously as I'd hoped she would. We stood just a step away from the hot rain pelting the submissive world, until I realized my grandmother stood at my elbow very much as God seemed always to do.

"What are you two laughing about?" she demanded.

It was the kind of interrogatory I figured meant she'd heard the whole thing, plus she had her "I heard the whole thing" face on.

Cece folded immediately, not that I was surprised by that. She pointed at me. "Archy said…"

I was still smarting from whatever punishment I honestly now don't remember I got for this on the night I came out to the kitchen again, this time to find Cece in high distress. "I have to go bad!" she whispered. "And Nicky just got in the bathroom and I can't hold it!"

It's a powerful and beautiful thing when your compassion and vengeance are aroused in the same circumstance, because you can tell yourself candidly that you are simply acting in the other person's best interest, even when that person is the one who normally makes you want to smash things with her hateful pestering and diabolical gift for sabotage.

"Well," I said after a moment's malicious deliberation, "you *could* go in the sink."

"Nuh-UH!" she whispered again, more frantically than before. But the thing that takes over a person—sometimes a lust for vengeance and conquest and sometimes nothing at all—had gotten me but good. I persisted, simultaneously fascinated by the situation and my own insane reaction to it.

"Why not?" I countered now. "We can rinse it out right away. Just do it really fast."

It was one of those pure and beautiful moments when, even though you know God is two rooms away in the living room watching Ted Mack's Amateur Hour, you are alone in a godless universe about to instigate the commission of a godless act but perfectly willing to accept and hang the consequences, when the consequences, even if they still seem likely, appear breathless, stunning, magnificent.

And by now Cece was becoming convinced by my air of reckless authority. Besides, her situation was clearly getting the best of her. I mapped out the plan: she would pull her pants down, and I would lift her up to the sink and she would go while I turned my head away. Beyond that, I really hadn't thought out the rest of the mechanics—how to wipe, how to flush—but I must have figured those would take care of themselves. Even so, we bickered another half minute until something about her dependent need must have finally broken through to me. I'm not positive what I felt when I recognized it, but I think by then I'd forgotten all about revenge. I may have felt benevolent toward her. I may have felt a surge of the white-hot anger that often hit me when she wanted me to mother her. Whichever it was, I wavered and she dug in her heels.

"I can't!" she whimpered.

By now, though, I saw that time was going to run out one way or the other, and seeing that, I took out the ace I still held up my sleeve.

"Look," I said. "You can't wet your pants."

That did it; she was terrified; I had her. We both took a deep breath, and she pulled down her pants, jumping up and down with her legs pressed together, her pants and underpants around her ankles, me grabbing her under the arms. Neither of us was particularly embarrassed yet, as I remember it. I know I was as fascinated by random nakedness as the average eleven-year-old, but this was a view of something I had changed in and out of bathing suits next to since I could remember. No, our terror was the improvised toilet behind us that we were going to have to watch my grandmother wash dishes in for the rest of our lives. Still, the situation was real and it was desperate, and neither of us was any longer in any position to cavil over necessity.

But we'd already run out of time, of course: my grandmother walked in on us just as I was just about to lift Cece up, and of course she didn't see me lifting Cece, she just saw us standing together, me towering over Cece with my pants on, Cece looking up to me with hers pulled down.

"What are you *doing*?" Grandma screamed, vibrating with outrage. I turned to her, not truly surprised—she was nearly always vibrating with outrage—but convinced I could easily explain the logic of the proceedings, and possibly even wrap things up so satisfactorily I would feature as the heroine of the tableau.

"Well, Nicky is in the bathroom," I began in a mockery of glib confidence that I could tell immediately by the absolute non-diminution of outrage was the wrong posture to assume. I temporized, certain I could explain everything so that she would understand that, even though I would shortly be very willing to express my gratitude to her for saving me from a serious misjudgment, I could easily explain my motives, after which she would be as delighted as I to have everything straightened out so perfectly. Cece, it would be clearly understood, had put me in an impossible position, and I was doing my best to deal with it honorably while sparing anyone else inconvenience. The mere fact that I was thinking this elaborately was a testimony to the terror I felt. But I had to make a push to save face, at the very least, even if death were to follow, which seemed likely. When I finished sputtering out some version of this rationale, it was immediately clear that I had not yet begun to misjudge the situation.

"How *dare* you!" she spat at me.

I still don't know if Cece had wet herself by this time or if her need to go had been cauterized by shock. She'd started crying the minute my grandmother came in the room, not that I blamed her, but I really don't remember whether she ran from the room, whether my grandmother sent her out, or what the end of the story was for her. She became a fiction the minute my grandmother put her to rights and turned back to me.

I wasn't surprised that she was angry—after all, someone had been just about to pee in her sink—but I was astonished at the rage she was in, and that it was turned on me. For it was clear Cece was in no trouble at all, which I still could not understand. To this point I'd been so busy trying to excuse myself I hadn't really had the guts to look closely at her, but now there was no place else to look. We stood alone in the kitchen, facing off. And I then saw in her such disgust as I'd not seen before anywhere, and seeing it showed me what she thought I had been about to do.

And I couldn't believe it. I couldn't speak. I wanted to murder Cece, and Nicky, and every bad stroke of luck that had made me waltz into the kitchen that night. I wanted to vomit. I waited for her to slap me, or at least spank me so I'd have a reason to hit her back. I'd never felt that before in my life, and I didn't care. But nothing happened.

Because then she just seemed defeated—incensed and outraged still, to be sure, but defeated by the magnitude of my supposed treachery, which seemed to have taken on a body in the room with us, one too big for her to subjugate. I began to feel its reality and solidity, and my rage turned to shame in that instantaneous way it does when you're that young and can't quite think things all the way through and when you've already had a lifetime of practice at making that switch. My guilt was before me, anyway: I knew I'd started the whole thing to punish Cece, and if this was the outcome I furiously admitted I might deserve it, however extraneous the outcome was to the facts. I also still believed that when she had time to reflect she couldn't possibly think so badly of me. Could she?

Finally she said, "You. Of all people." It wasn't an acknowledgment of my innocence, but it was a gesture of repair, I knew that, and I was grateful for it. Next to the horror I could read the relief that by the grace of God she'd stopped me from doing the unthinkable, and that I'd been saved from myself, saved from committing an evil she could imagine but believed I could not.

I was banished to my room for the rest of the night, of course. I remember the heaviness of going up the back stairs as the relief of her small gesture faded, leaving me with the weight of this terrible thing that hadn't been anywhere near my mind. I don't remember much else except that I lay on the bed, not bothering to turn on the lamp, the dark deepening until everyone else came up for the night. My grandmother must have shooed me into my pyjamas and had me brush my teeth, but I don't remember that either. I'm not sure now why I thought it might come, but I know I waited for an apology; still, for the rest of that night she acted as if nothing had happened. And in her universe, that was the one sure sign that something had.

I remember how long I lay on top of the bed spread that night, trembling with what she'd imagined I had done. *It wasn't me*, I muttered as I lay there. *That wasn't me.*

MON DEYE MON – NADINE PINEDE

My mother's stories are always dressed up as proverbs. *Deye mon gen mon*, is her favorite. "Beyond mountains, there are mountains." For us Haitians, there's always a mountain of trouble waiting up the path, yet music and laughter fill the valley beneath. I learn to listen when the women tell stories in the kitchen. Sometimes they send me away. These are stories for *gran moun*, my mother says. Wait until you're older.

We live in Montreal. Around me, I hear two tongues. One is the French of Quebec. The other is Kreyol, the language of my parents' native land. Haiti is a place they love, but it's also a place where the President for Life has the Ton Ton Macoutes, who wear sunglasses and dark suits and can make people disappear.

I have Gilberte to keep me safe when my parents are at work. We found her through our Church. She is a big woman, with stiff red hair and skin that is fish-belly-white. She was born and raised in the Laurentian Mountains near Montreal, where the villages are named after saints. I love her because she doesn't have to love me, yet it's obvious she does.

One afternoon when I should be napping, I peek into Gilberte's room. She is doing her rosary with her eyes closed. Her scalp is eggshell smooth; her red hair sits on a faceless foam head. I back away quietly. Our secret.

We move from Montreal to Guelph, a small prairie town in Ontario. Gilberte is sick so she can't come with us. We must leave her behind, just as we leave a place where everyone speaks French and I have friends. Winter lasts longer here. I sink into snowdrifts with each step I take to school.

At St. Francis of Assisi, the nuns teach me cursive letters, and Peter, with straw blonde hair and rusty freckles, calls me a nigger. It's a new word for me, and I have to ask my mother what it means. I always knew we were Haitian, but now we're the only Black people in town.

Language makes us different too. I'd rather be silent than make a mistake. My drawings are my voice. I draw a picture of our house covered in snow with a curl of smoke in the chimney. The teacher picks it out as the best in class and asks who drew it.

I raise my hand. All eyes are on me. "That is my house." My first English words out loud. I am surprised by the fierce sound of my own voice in this foreign tongue, how clotted it is with the desire to speak. If Gilberte could see me now.

But now I'm alone. My mother asks our neighbor's son to babysit while she learns English at night school. This boy, who once helped me when my numb hands fumbled with the house key, is the same one who blindfolds me and ties me up with my mother's stocking. He says we will play a special game.

The snakes in my nightmares wake me up. I wet my pants in school, and they complain I stink of piss. *Don't tell*, he warned me, but I did. He is told to stay away. He is not reported to the police. Years later, when I asked my mother why, she said: *Deye mon gen mon. Of course I believed you, but who would have believed us? We were strangers in their land.*

EGGS – SUSAN WHITE

My mother's hatred for her sister goes back to the chicken. An Easter chick dyed cotton candy blue. My mother told me this story to squash my fondness for my aunt, Big Joan.

Under the oppressive Tennessee sun, the two girls in their homemade white dresses spent the afternoon in their backyard playing with their chicks. Probably because she handled it too much—and because of the chemicals saturating its miniature body—Joan's green chick swooned into a limp death before supper. After the burial behind the swing set, Joan stood on top of the rust-red picnic table glaring down at my mother's chick, Lucy, that pecked each speck on the smooth, cement sidewalk. My mom squatted by the screen door, calling Lucy as if she were a dog. The chick cocked its head toward the noise and shrugged its wing-nubs. Joan jumped from the table. The bones popped and crunched. Thick darkness leaked from the blue beneath Joan's new Sunday shoes.

So what came before the chicken? An egg. And then a zygote. And then a child. But then another child. And they are sisters, right? Same last name, dark hair, nose, and accent.

But, according to my mother, they had nothing but differences on the inside. She insists that Joan ruined her childhood. My mom learned not to count her chicks, lest they be flattened beneath the fierce foot of her selfish sister.

When I was old enough to grow my own eggs and to know that parents cry and lie, I asked Joan how she remembered the Easter deaths. She claimed the unfortunate blue chick's demise was an accident. With a brash smoker's laugh, she said, "Your mother is the victim in all her stories." She stood, running her hands down her thighs, smoothing her linen pants. "And I'm always the villain." Winking at me, she added, "Some people need a villain to explain their failures."

I cannot help but admire Joan's certainty. Her swaggering speech. She was, after all, a high school basketball star in the fifties who sported a flat-top.

Now she is a retired Personnel Director of the Arlington School System. She hatched no children. She is what no one talked about until I came right out and asked it: a lesbian.

I thought I was a boy the first few years of my life. Born between brothers, I wore my hair short, played shirtless and shoeless in the neighborhood, and tried to pee standing up. My mother called me to the Formica kitchen table. Showed me a picture book and gave me an anatomy lesson. I believed she cast a spell on me with strange, magical words to turn me into a girl that day. But I was four and incapable of understanding a halved sandwich was the same amount as one sandwich. A few weeks earlier, I had dropped a large rock on the malfunctioning TV left in our yard to release all the characters. After epic battles of forcing party dresses over my head, my mother eventually convinced me I was born a female.

When I was seven, another girl insisted upon being born into our family. After my mom's life-threatening delivery and two cesarean deliveries, a doctor cut three and a half inches off my mother's fallopian tube and then knotted her femininity. But my mother grew a new tube, which a fertilized egg traveled down—becoming my sister.

Because my father had a pregnant wife and three kids, my mother's mother stayed with us. We ate from covered dishes that neighbors and friends delivered. And my grandmother drew a picture of a uterus and fetus to explain a different kind of *delivery* to my brothers and me. My older brother left the room when she said the word *vagina*. Before bed, Grandmother Dale made us pray that our mother and the baby would be all right. "Deliver us from evil," we had learned to recite in our Episcopal church.

Easter came before my sister. The night before the first ovulating moon of spring, my swollen mother hid eggs around our front yard. The next morning, three eager kids grabbed the baskets filled with green plastic grass that lay waiting for us on the living room floor. We ran down the unswept, stone steps into our yard, which was littered with dyed egg shells and chocolate wrappers. Our dogs had found the hidden treasures first. A couple of days later, one of those dogs, a chow-shepherd mix with a half-black tongue, killed the rabbit our uncle gave us. Slung it around and snapped its neck. It was a limp Easter. The next Easter, partly out of curiosity and partly out of revenge, I built a trap for the Easter Bunny. I dug a hole, put carrots in the bottom of it, and covered it. The only thing I caught was a spanking for digging up our side yard.

On Earth Day Anne was born yellow. Her blood rebelled against my mother's. Anne and my father were whisked off to Nashville so someone else's blood could be siphoned into the side of her soft head. Meanwhile, the surgeon removed part of my mother's uterus. The stitching busted. Her pulse lowered, and gas could not escape her body. She lay there with a tube in every orifice. In Nashville, my father sat in a hospital chair wearing sterilized clothes, holding his baby, 90 miles from his struggling wife. My mother pulled through and came home two days before Anne. I was allowed to hold my sister before either of my brothers did.

Anne always knew she was a girl. She sprouted fiery hair, rekindled from two generations past on my mother's side, which her green and yellow dresses complemented. She delighted my grandmother by actually taking the dolls she gave her out of the box. (There is a Christmas picture of me aiming my brother's bee-bee gun at a doll standing upright in its package.)

In our house, we could dial 8-1 and hang up to make all the phones ring. Our house was old and sprawling, so this trick allowed us to be lazy and informed. We rang for wake-up calls, meal times, homework questions, and just to see who was there and who wasn't. It did not take me long to learn how to abuse this system. Rather than making crank calls to strangers, I made my voice strange to fool my family. Eventually, I came up with the idea of *faux*-calls: answering my own ring and feigning a conversation. On one particular afternoon when I was babysitting my six-year-old sister, I allowed her to make Kool-Aid/cookie/whipped cream treats. As she laid the soggy concoctions on aluminum foil, I furtively dialed 8-1 on the filthy kitchen phone and hung up. Anne lifted her little red head to watch me answer the phone. "Hello," I said. "Oh, hi. I'm fine. Babysitting my sister. . . . yes . . . . let me see. . ." I pulled the long, spiraled cord behind me as I walked to the refrigerator, opened it, and looked inside. "Yes, we have eggs . . . . Sure. I'll send my sister over . . . . No problem." Anne, kneeling in the ripped vinyl chair, was obviously curious about what I had volunteered her for. "That was Mrs. Hibberts from next door. She's making a cake but just realized she doesn't have any eggs. She needs you to take her three eggs."

Anne frowned. "You take them." She was terribly shy, and I was terribly wily.

I pressed on. "She asked for you to bring them because she found something in her attic that she thought you would like. A surprise."

Through the dining room window, I watched Anne take careful steps toward the neighbor's side door. She cradled the eggs against her pudgy belly. She rang the doorbell. Mr. Hibberts opened the door. Anne talked. He leaned down to hear her better. Then turned back inside the house. Mrs. Hibberts appeared and smiled down at Anne who held the eggs out to her. Mrs. Hibberts accepted the offering from the tiny mystic. Anne walked back empty-handed, disappointed that Mrs. Hibberts had decided not to give her a surprise.

Anne will be married this spring. She plans to have children. I have wandered the wilderness for nearly forty years, yet I have no children. When I was thirty, I considered selling my eggs. I discovered that my eggs were five years beneath the cut-off age and rapidly depreciating. I also found out that the value of my eggs would be assessed according to my height, SAT scores, athleticism, and health. The process, I was also told, is painful. I opted to keep my eggs, more to avoid the ego pain of finding out my monetary value than avoiding the physical pain I would endure.

Tomorrow is Easter. Julia and I will put chicken and ham inside plastic eggs and hide them around the yard. This time they are meant for our dogs—who will sniff them out. Roll them with their noses. Crack them open with their teeth. Eat the meat and lick the plastic.

We all find our way to prevent the Humpty Dumpty tragedy.

SHE LEADS ME – MARJORIE SAISER

She leads me to the place under the trees
where her father, years ago,
fell dead

beside the buzz saw,
the broken blade in his throat.
Spot of grass where he lay

when she ran from the house to the grove and saw him.
Will you stay with the body? someone asked her,
and she did.

She knelt beside the body, laid her apron over his face.
The body dressed as it was in chore clothes, layers
of shirts, heavy coat.

No gloves, the better to guide the wood
to the blade. The body
needing work, needing cattle,

a horse to ride, a barn to build,
as if work were food and drink:
lift this, carry this, never put it down.

The body, marvelous when bending,
beautiful carrying, kneeling, hammering,
exquisite the movement, the dance.

Her hands on my shoulders, she turns me to face her.
You can always, she tells me--
her lips pursing and flexing and her teeth small, gray—

you can always do what you have to do.

HEAT – MICHELLE CACHO-NEGRETE

The heat, that summer of 1957, was a dense web that draped New York with the particular hazy dreaminess of an impressionist painting. I was thirteen and had my first job, stapling tags onto winter clothes in the warehouse of a department store. My mother worked as a file clerk in Manhattan for fifty dollars a week after my father deserted her, my brother and me.

My mother and I would travel together on the train. That first morning sweat dripped down my back.

"I don't remember heat like this," Mother said solemnly.

My stop came first and she nudged me toward the door. "Have a good day. Work hard."

An attractive, middle-aged black woman with conked hair, brown-rimmed glasses, and mauve lipstick greeted me at the warehouse door, held out a callused hand, offered, "I'm Alice. Come meet the boss."

I followed her to a small, air-conditioned office. The man behind the desk looked through me as though I was transparent.

He said, "Well Michelle, work hard." His absent-minded dismissal of me, relegating me into the anonymous pool of another poor kid working in a warehouse somehow electrified me. I knew at that moment that, as an adult I would work for myself despite the odds against it.

The warehouse ran the length of the building. Since factories worked one season ahead, it swirled with wool clothing. A few tall floor fans were scattered around, but each row of clothes was so narrow that a fanned breeze didn't stand a chance of penetrating. I was given a fat chrome machine on wheels to staple the price on each item.

I remember the name of only one co-worker: Mary.

Her brown hair was wild. Her eyes were slanted in the manner that indicates Down syndrome. Her mouth was blindingly scarlet, white teeth ruffled with lipstick. She was in her late twenties with slouching shoulders and a full, fine body. She offered an enormous smile and a poorly articulated "Hello." I answered, "Hi," and smiled back.

"Get to work, Mary," Alice said.

As Mary turned away I said, "My name is Michelle. Pleased to meet you, Mary." She flashed another quick smile then with a glance at Alice began stapling with a practiced, smooth precision.

Each morning I exchanged hellos with Mary, touched by her quiet shyness. Her work was fast and perfect. Every day before lunch the boss checked up on The Floor and one particular afternoon, I heard him growl, "You're a bad girl, Mary. No lunch today."

I was astonished as I watched her shuffle like a frightened mouse to some suits against the farthest wall.

Alice called for lunch then and the click of machines halted like a field of crickets gone dead. I paused when I passed her, frightened by her cross look. I thought of Mary without a respite from the deadening heat and stuttered, "The boss told Mary she couldn't go out on lunch. Isn't that illegal?" I was embarrassed at the nervous break in my voice.

She stared at me impassively then said, "He's the boss." She straightened up and walked toward the door. "He knows what's legal. Keep your nose out of it."

I flushed brick red and joined my co-workers outside as we opened our sandwich bags and cans of soda. I discovered, however, that I'd left my cigarettes in my purse and went back to get it.

I swung open the warehouse door. The dense heat inside closed around me like a trap. A soft whimpering from a row near the back wall stopped me. I peeked between a row of long green coats where Mary sat, legs sprawled, face mottled with sweat and tears, eyes screwed shut. The boss stood over her, narrow shoulders outlined by the wet shirt clinging to his back. He turned, zipping his fly, face expressionless. I began to shake as he strode away. I shivered violently understanding what had happened, might be regularly happening.

I ran to find Alice, stood before her sweat dripping down my face, and whispered, "Mary, the boss, he's…"

She scowled at me. "Mind your own business, girl," then walked off.

Over the next month I had nightmares; flashes of Mary's face lipstick-stained and blotched, the boss's body engulfing hers. Who could actually help some retarded worker in a shit-waged job? In desperation, I tried to speak with Alice again.

She curved into herself like a turtle and snapped, "Mary needs this job. It's the boss keeps her here. You want to get her fired?"

I walked away from Alice, aware then of life's varying shades of gray.

Alice deviated from her position only once. Mary had a bad cold; her face flushed enough to suggest a fever. When the boss appeared, Alice called sharply, "Mary, come here and help me carry these boxes out." He spun and stared at her, but she met his eyes full on and he stayed away the rest of the week.

I woke up every morning feeling like a wild animal was trapped inside me, struggling to break out. One morning on the train, I asked, "Ma, what can you do if somebody thinks they're doing something wrong."

She looked at me and asked, "You've done something wrong?" "No," I said hastily. "I just wondered. How do you make it right?"

She leaned closer, her lips against my ear, so that I might hear her over the roaring of the train. "You often can't make right what you did wrong, but you try to do better.."

"What if you don't think you can do better, if it seems impossible?" I thought of my father's desertion, my mother's low paying job, Mary's helplessness, and blurted out, "It's such a bad world. How can you do anything?"

She shook her head. Anger mingled with sadness, filled her eyes. "It's impossible to change the world. You pick your battles. Figure out which ones you stand a chance of winning and then just let go of the rest. Try to improve things in your little world. That's the best you can do."

On the last day of work, Alice shook my hand, looked at me appraisingly then asked, "What's the cheapest commodity in the world?"

I shrugged. "Candy?"

She threw her head back and laughed a little too wildly. When she stopped, her eyes were wet. "We are," she told me. "We are."

ASCETICISM – REBECCA LAUREN

My mother skipped the word *relations*
when she read the Old Testament out loud before bed

and I wondered what Tamar and Judah planned to do
with each other that made her twist her face when she came

to verse sixteen, as if the milk in her glass had gone sour
on the tongue. I gathered that sex was something that went dark

when the lights went out, the way my mother's glass of milk, if left
on the nightstand, turned gray with shadow long after

the passage was read, the Bible returned to its shelf. Most nights,
I'd take it down again, search with flashlight beneath blankets

for mention of bodies or liquid or beds. God, it seemed,
was the only one who wasn't afraid to say that semen spilled,

that breasts rolled like gazelles in open fields, that the union of flesh
was warm, wet, vital. He made me thirsty, made me grope for a sip

of milk before sleep. And when I reached, groggy,
for the glass in the dark, when soggy shadows began pooling

in all directions and I heard my own muffled cry, I knew to wait
for the flash of light, the glints of glass in a white pool on the bedroom floor,

a woman on her knees at the door with a wet rag, whispering *hush*.

BAND PRACTICE – ANNE PEKURI

During fourth grade music class, 1960, Mrs. Peden placed a 78 record on the portable turntable. As it began to spin she said, "Children, this is a musical version of *Peter and the Wolf*. Each character in the story is represented by one of the instruments you see in the pictures hanging above the blackboard."

I recognized some of them. My biggest brother, Bobby, played the French horn and my mother played the saxophone.

Carefully, Mrs. Peden set the player's needle into the vinyl groove and looked us over with a light in her eyes. The music began and she whispered, "Now, children, which instrument do you think is making *this* sound?"

That winter, Mrs. Peden had us draw and color each of the instruments she'd introduced. We wrote about the wood and metals from which they were made, how they were crafted and the history of each. We learned what made them sing.

After four years of playing in the elementary and middle school bands, I entered Glenrock high school and the high school band. As lower classmen, we were issued the left-over sizes of purple and white wool uniforms with gilt and tassels, hats with black patent brims and bright buttons, pants with razor sharp creases and piping down the side seams.

Early on day one of our freshman year marching band practice for football season was scheduled for the first period and began in the music room. Above the cacophony of talking, scraping chairs and instrument tuning our director, Mr. Jackson, tapped his wand on the podium and called over our heads. "Here, here, everyone."

When the din lessoned, he added, "I want to see you all in front of the school in five minutes, tuned and ready to go. Pick up a sheet of each of these five pieces—KEEP THEM IN THIS ORDER—and put them in your clips."

I had never worn the music holder attached to my clarinet and it added weight, even without the music.

Gathered in front of the school on Third Street, just two blocks from my house, Mr. Jackson called us to order, "Flutes, in front. Clarinets and Ruth (she played the oboe). Saxes and trombones next. Trumpets and baritone! Tubas and drummers, take the rear." We were six rows deep and five wide.

I was in the second row on the end, next to Carolyn, on my left. A sophomore, she wore her hair cut above her ears. Freckles dappled her pointy nose and when she smiled, everyone looked twice to see if they were the lucky recipients. I got to know her profile well. She had the ability to speak out of the corner of her mouth like a cartoon character.

"Everyone!" Mr. Jackson raised and waved his staff before us, his voice strained. The older classmen stood at ease, resting their instruments comfortably. Mine felt cumbersome.

"Everyone!" he repeated. "Arms' length apart, front, sideways and back."

Frosty, a six foot five inch, two hundred pound freshman who played the tuba immediately knocked little Danny Daniels into a neighboring drummer.

"Now, look down your rows. You shouldn't be able to see anyone except the person next to you. If you do, you're out of line. Fix it!"

There was much jostling and joking.

Mr. Jackson turned his back to us, long staff high in the air, and tweeted his whistle. "Twwee-et."

The older classmen immediately brought their feet together and stood at attention.

"Tweet!"

Snare drums began a roll.

The older classmen began marching in place. Left. Left. Left right left.

"Tweet!"

The older classmen moved forward and the rest of us jumped to keep from being hit from behind. The bass drum began: Boom! Boom! Boom, boom, boom!

Carolyn joined the bass drum, chanting out of the corner of her mouth on my behalf, "Left. Left. Left, right, left!" as she emphasized the pattern with her left foot.

I hopped and jumped trying to match her steps.

Across the street, the beat of drums brought Mrs. Lindsay, our retired school nurse, to her front step.

As I watched Carolyn to see how she carried her clarinet, Mr. Jackson's whistle blew and she raised it to her lips. Another whistle and she began to play. Playing while sitting in a chair in the music room is different than playing while walking, much less, marching. We were *supposed* to lift our thighs parallel to the ground, pointing our toes downward. My teeth bumped the mouthpiece and pinched my upper lip. Not the only one to emit squeaks and squawks, I was so out of breath and rhythm I couldn't play. I hoped Carolyn hadn't noticed.

By the second repeat of the refrain I could play a few notes. Then, I saw my row was rippled and I got out of step trying to line up.

Before we reached the end of the block, the widow, Mrs. Epperly, and our school maintenance man and his wife, watched from their porches. Out for their morning constitutional, the principal, Mr. Rock, and his wife, stopped on the sidewalk, smiling and waving. Ruth's wire-haired terrier appeared, weaving in and out of our ranks. He got so excited when he found her that he jumped at her for a full block and her face turned as red as her hair.

We marched on down Third Street toward Main Street, past my old baby sitter's. She stood in her yard, across the fence from a buxom woman who eyed us sharply and I wondered, not for the first time, why everyone called her Pinkie.

We marched past the elementary school where tiny brothers and sisters waited in the schoolyard for the first bell to ring. They lined the fence to watch. Some of the girls had band-aids on their knobby knees and the boys wore their pants at the high-water mark or rolled into bulky cuffs. Some called our names and waved their fingers through the cyclone webbing.

We marched past the post office where the Post Mistress's spectacles reflected behind the multi-paned window. Cars pulled over to let us pass. Women, wearing drapes with hair partially done, came out of the beauty shop and suddenly, we were at Main Street and faced with a turn--it was a left turn, not that it mattered. Some of us didn't know in advance that the inside of a curve is shorter than the outside, the inner rows needed to march in place as the outer rows opened their strides. A saxophonist hopped out of line after a trumpeter stepped on his heel. Pulling the strap over his head, he handed his sax to a man who'd just come out of the bar and then, sat on the curb to put his shoe back on. By the time we passed the service station, where the attendant covered his eyes from the sun, we were all out of step and even the upper classmen were confused.

Mr. Jackson marched proudly on in front of us, his staff beating the air triumphantly. Now that we were downtown and the street was lined with early shoppers and shopkeepers, he tweeted his whistle again.

This time we were ready. Or thought we were. Most of us newcomers had forgotten to rotate our music and a few sheets fluttered to the road.

I had a chip in my reed. Replacements were a dollar fifty.

Carolyn started choking and now was giggling into her clarinet. It was obvious Mr. Jackson had gotten carried away. We sounded terrible and reached the next turn, onto Fourth Street, before we finished playing the march. We freshman just quit trying, which was probably just as well. We made the second turn without losing any shoes, though I wouldn't have called it *marching* either.

At last, we were on the home stretch, back to school. I wanted to run; but people lined the street. My lip swelled and my thumb felt numb from the weight of the clarinet.

The butcher came out the side door of the Corner Market, removing his apron, as my old piano teacher came out of her family's publishing company. She wore a silky purple dress and held her hand over her heart (which she did even while teaching me piano). I could smell her perfume from the street.

Inside the picture window in Quentin Hooley's drug store, Herb and Dave, two of our trombonists, each held an instrument in one hand and a glass of soda in the other, which they raised, as though toasting us. Carolyn said, "Smart-asses! Don't look. Ignore them." They must have slipped from our ranks and cut through the elementary school playground to race ahead and taunt us.

As we passed the far side of the elementary school grounds, a jangly bell rang and the children ran through the school doors like marbles funneled into a bag. Beyond that, Fourth Street was quieter, with less of an audience.

Herb and Dave returned noisily, though Mr. Jackson seemed not to notice. As soon as we reached the back of the high school, his whistle tweeted. The upper classmen marched in place and we ran into them.

"Twee-et!"

Drums sounded a roll and the whistle tweeted again. The upper classmen's feet stopped. What relief!

Mr. Jackson remained a moment, straight back sagging. When he turned, shaking his head, he looked deflated. "All right, people. Tomorrow, I want you lined up and ready to march at 8:10, sharp. You may go!"

We flew.

KEROSENE – JULIE HENSLEY

A Summer after sixteen others, unfurls slowly.
I pick Japanese beetles from tomato plants
as the cat winds a warm dust-cover around my ankles,
seal each shimmery insect in a jar of kerosene.
I smell raked alfalfa cooking in the fields.
My legs swing from the tailgate
as the world rushes by in a shudder of loose gravel.

At night, the boy peels clothing away fragrantly
like pieces of orange,
and I move beneath him inside the sleeping bag,
something almost ready to hatch.
Desire settles in my stomach, thick like pond debris,
and I whisper
don't stop.
But far below, in the valley porch lights wink,
and there is the sound of midnight rigs on Route 33,
distant bees calling me back.

In August, from the porch swing
I watch that calf skid away from its mother, like laughter
skipping through ragweed and clumps of dry orchard grass
to lodge its neck, firmly, in a rusty hayrake
half-hidden by thistle.
Unnerved by the new weight,
it bolts for the pond.
My father and the farmer across the road come running,
but it's too late
to pull the thing out alive.

YARD WORK – KATHLEEN LYNCH

My mother prowled the yard, winding wires around bare
stems of rose bushes, attaching Woolworth's plastic roses—
her flowered house dress puffed out full,
hair lifting like flames. I watched, embarrassed

by how tacky, how pathetic
but it had been a bad spring all around
what with Dad's drinking and with nothing
blooming, and from where I stood

I had to admit they looked pretty. The distance
between shame and pride is so mutable we use
both words for the same thing:
She has no shame. She has no pride.

Can this be true? By my calculation over forty
thousand hours have passed since that moment
and still I see her and the bell of that dress,
not a scrim in sight, just sheets snapping

on the line behind her, weeds shivering at her ankles.
And the way she moved, the way she went at it
—a driven thing—another of the countless gestures
she would subsume in silence, a look

in the eye we all knew meant: Say nothing.
And when she sank away into the heap of mystery
books on the couch, a theater of colors in the window
behind her—the strange brilliance and juxtaposition

of fake and real—I began to believe in hope
as something that could be invented
even under dire skies, even when wind
sliced around thorns and we waited

for the phone to ring, and for spring
to become spring.

TITLE IX AND ME – NANCY MCKINLEY

Twenty-five men in Speedos flanked the coach. They frowned and stared at me, the lone female, as I walked into the pool area that first day of swim team. Thanks to Title IX, College of the Holy Cross had gone coed that year. As one of only a hundred women in the first female class of 1976, I had almost adjusted to being the only female in my academic classes, but not in a swimming pool, and certainly not in a bathing suit.

How could I explain I had no interest in competing against males? They stood twice my size and sped halfway down the pool before I dove off the starting block. I simply wanted to improve my times and stay in shape. Plus, I knew the importance of athletic participation. If females failed to demonstrate interest, we might lose our hard-won access.

As I swam my warm-up laps, some guys *accidentally* hit me in the face; a few others kicked me during flip turns. They didn't want me sharing *their* pool. Their response smacked of the welcome I had received from my humanities classes. Each time I spoke, I heard *Dumb Broad* or *Smart Bitch*, followed by jokes about the inferiority of the female brain. The laughter never included mine.

At the end of practice, Coach gathered us for a talk. He seemed nice enough, but in today's world, we'd say he needed sensitivity training. After taking sizes for team suits, he said, "Your suit will cost three times as much as theirs." I pointed out he only needed to buy one, and he smiled. But when I asked about using the locker room, he showed me the janitor's closet. Coach knew I wouldn't want the guys to wait while I showered and changed.

With a bucket and mop serving as my clothes tree, I wriggled out of my suit, and then showered at my dormitory. The process became routine, but not my presence. After meets, if a swimmer performed poorly, Coach ordered him to practice in my training circle. Naturally I considered quitting, but a few swimmers offered encouragement.

Then came a defining moment. We traveled to an away meet at an all male college where the host team directed me to a locker room. Apparently as

I changed, they tried to enter, but my teammates blocked their access. I suppose a shift had taken place, but none of us had realized it. For the next few weeks, practices continued with an emphasis on an Invitational scheduled for later that month. We arrived at the important weekend when key swimmers came down with the flu. Coach shook his head and put me on the medley relay. Amazingly we did well enough to score points needed to win the meet, and that meant the entire team would receive trophies at the end of the season.

The team banquet, a dressy occasion, took place on campus. Many of the swimmers brought dates, so my appearance seemed less noticeable than at practice. Coach made a speech and recognized the seniors and top performers. Before handing out awards, he opened the box that held our trophies. Suddenly his face grew pale. He looked out over the team and fixed his gaze on me. Then Coach laughed, "I guess we'll all remember the year the team went coed!" For some reason, a mix-up had occurred: the box held twenty-five female trophies and one male trophy.

DEAL WITH IT MADAME – HUDA AL-MARASHI

By the time I'd reached the final pages of Gustave Flaubert's classic paperback, I'd had enough of Madame Bovary. The entire novel, the nineteenth-century protagonist's incessant whining had annoyed me. She married a boring man, but a decent one, hardworking and loyal. And now I couldn't believe the ending I was reading. Suicide. It was far too drastic an end for far too common a problem.

So what if she didn't love her husband?

I lay on my bed in my dorm-room and tried to figure out how I was going to write an academic paper on this character without sounding like a budding fundamentalist. Madame Bovary was a sinner and an adulterer, a victim of western society and all its fixed notions about love. Westerners had to have attraction and chemistry for the duration of a relationship. My mother had warned me not to succumb to this foolishness. Love grew over time as long as you didn't ask too much from it. Clearly, Emma had wanted too much from her 1850s world. It was 1996, and almost every woman in my family had married their Charles. None of them had affairs or tried to kill themselves.

At office hours the next day, I admitted to my professor that I'd been struggling with the topic. "I'm choosing to live that life. I'm engaged now, and I don't think Madame Bovary had to do any of the things she did."

Dr. Martin looked at me, with what I told myself was interest rather than concern, and invited me out to dinner. The following week, we slid into a booth at the campus café. "So tell me about your engagement," Dr. Martin said, a grainy sandwich in her hands.

Normally, this question would've pushed me into a conversational boxing stance. I was convinced that people outside the Muslim world assumed I had been promised since birth and that it was my job to show them otherwise. But that night, Dr. Martin's question struck me as chatty, as something two adults would say to each other. And so I replied, "I got engaged in November to the son of family friends. Our dads went to medical school together in Baghdad. And he'd always liked me—"

I stopped. I was defending myself. Americans never said, "My fiancé likes me." That part went without saying.

"But you do know you don't have to do this?" Dr. Martin's tone was matter-of-fact, as if she was simply making sure I'd been informed.

I struggled to swallow the dry bread in my mouth and said, "Of course. This was my choice. I know my fiancé. Our parents didn't even really want us to get engaged now, but I was ready."

"I didn't mean to suggest anything," Dr. Martin said. "It's just that you're such a bright girl, and I'd hate to see this get in the way of your education."

I took a sip of my water and tried to come up with a way to explain what I was thinking: That Americans were wrong to assume marriage hindered a young person's future. Marriage marked the beginning of independent adulthood.

"It's not like that at all," I said. "Getting married will actually help me get to graduate school because my parents wouldn't let me live on my own otherwise."

I couldn't see how this small declaration of independence spoke a different truth. If Dr. Martin did, she didn't mention it. She stirred her soup and said, "I see your point, but marriage can be a struggle. I got married young. We had two small children, and I was trying to finish school. It wasn't easy, and we wound up getting divorced."

Dr. Martin had just given me permission to stop listening. Marriage might have been difficult for her because she had a white woman's expectations. I wanted to say, "We're different. You can walk away. I can't and I won't."

Instead I said, "But I expect it to be hard. That's the kind of marriages I know. You marry someone and you learn to love them. I guess that's why Madame Bovary bothers me. I think she should've been able to deal with it."

"So let's talk about Emma," Dr. Martin said, pushing her plate away. Emma, Dr. Martin explained, was profoundly influenced by romantic literature, the image of love as a whirlwind of unrelenting passion and desire. The romantic ideal of marriage bore little resemblance to the mundane reality of everyday life, and this devastated her.

This resonated with the romantic-comedy viewer in me to an extent I thought best left unacknowledged. But that afternoon, alone in my room, the thoughts I had tried to ignore during dinner with Dr. Martin resurfaced. I tapped my pen on the paper in front of me and admitted this: It was one thing to accept a certain societal position for women, another thing to be that woman, torn between what you wanted and what you believed you had to do.

Now that I'd arrived at this state of mind, I couldn't escape it. My hands scrawled out an essay sympathetic to Emma Bovary, to the tensions I could no longer deny. With college freshman wordiness, I wrote: "All over the world women continue to be challenged by the same war Emma Bovary was a casualty of. It is a do or die battle between what a woman knows she can do and what she is told she can do. According to Flaubert, 'a woman is constantly thwarted...there is always some desire urging her forward, always some convention holding her back.'"

A week later, I got my paper back. On the bottom, Dr. Martin wrote, "I am surprised by the radical critique of women's domestic roles that you make in light of our conversation." I put the paper in my binder and closed it. It felt as private as a journal entry, a confession that a part of me had come undone.

TEST GROUP FOUR: WOMANHOOD AND OTHER FAILURES – SJ SINDU

My love affair with women started when I learned about the female suicide bombers in Sri Lanka. I was five. It blew my mind that women—the make-upped, dark-eyed beauty queens of the Indian Bollywood movies—could be dangerous enough to strap on explosives beneath the folds of their sarees.

My lover's scar is crocheted through his chest with baby pink yarn by someone who was just learning. The scar runs through like a tiny mountain range stretching from armpit to armpit along the line of his pectoral muscles but never syncing with the contours of his body. When the surgeon scooped out the breast tissue he left my lover's chest flat.

The scar is pink like his nipples, soft and spongy where it bubbled up from the stitches and healed around them. Sometimes he's afraid he'll catch his nipples on something and rip them off. He has nightmares in which he is nipple-less.

There is a dark spot where his nipples used to be, a sunset gradation of color into the scar. Dark hairs sprout around the scar line, tall and curly. They weren't there before the testosterone. They grow a forest over his chest and down his stomach.

The outer edges of his scar bulge out in dog ears, a side effect of having had large breasts.

His lovers, the ones he used to have before me, wouldn't look at his chest. They would turn away, talk down into their coffee, tuck their hair behind their ears. They wouldn't touch him there, their fingers cringing from the ridges of the scar, their bodies shivering at the absence. He can't feel there anymore, numbness reaching up from his scar, a vacancy of nerves that feels hollow when he pushes on the skin. His lungs underneath can feel the pressure but the message of touch is lost between the skin and his insides.

My mother keeps a leather-bound album of my baby pictures tucked away in the recesses of her closet. These pictures are few, and it took years—decades—to collect them all in the volume. Most were lost to late night fleeings from our family home in Sri Lanka, where we always kept bags packed. The bags had to be light enough to carry for days, spare enough to unpack and repack at the Army checkpoints. Photo albums were treasured but bulky, and my baby pictures won out over my parents' wedding album. We were always ready to leave at notice that the battle line was nearing our town.

Now the pictures sleep peacefully in my mother's closet, trying to put their abandonment issues behind them. I've stolen a few photos of my own. I need to remember.

It's tempting to retell my childhood veiled in virginity, a chaste good Hindu girl's strict upbringing. But it's a little boy who stands in these pictures, one who was given too much freedom and adored to the point of exhaustion by extended family, before they remembered that he would bleed every month.

I had short curly hair and wore boy's clothes. In beach pictures I wear only my panties. I mourn the loss of that flat chest that allowed me to be rambunctious. Wild.

At six years old my best friend and I pretended to be Americans on vacation at a beach. We walked around in our panties inside locked rooms, windows shut for modesty. We played at being American women—smoking, drinking, kissing—unconstrained by sarees and rules.

To Emily Dickinson: I once met you—but you were dead—

To the middle-aged white lady who pretended to be Emily Dickinson at the library, and who I believed and loved until I told my friends and they made fun of me because I didn't know Emily Dickinson was dead and this lady was a fake: You were too pretty to play this part of lonely writer. I should've known. Even the Americans like their smart women ugly.

The dusty blue linoleum feels warm even though it snows outside. The tip of my nose is cold from the air. I lie against the warm floor, and the heat seeps in through the frilly cotton pajamas my mother made for me. My little brother laughs in the living room, his toddler voice hiccups around the walls as my dad plays with him. My mother types her thesis at the computer.

I lie on the warm linoleum to practice my drawing. Today I'm practicing lips, diligently consulting a three-ring binder of tutorials I have printed out from the Internet. I fill my papers with lips like the ones the tutorials show me, the round curves of women's lips that bite down on secrets and the flat plains of men's lips that don't smile.

I am in love with a man who doesn't believe in God, but believes that English majors and hippies are the fussy frou-frou in an otherwise functioning society. He teaches me how to catch and throw a softball, and buys me fountain pens and leather-bound journals. He tries to train our cat and when he can't, maintains that our cat over-generalizes. He lets me run my hands and lips along his chest scar, asks me to give him testosterone shots. I take pictures of the hairs that slowly explode on his jaw. Together we celebrate the dissolving curves of his body, my insides squirming at the woman slowly dying.

To my lover: Do you know, *kanna*, I learned about life from the female soldiers that patrolled my hometown. And about love, too. They had things figured out, their wisdoms wrapped away in the tight braids of their hair.

I see my best friend when I visit Sri Lanka after high school. We have seen eighteen from two different oceans. I wear makeup and short skirts in the Sri Lankan heat. She has hair braided down her back and makes tea for everyone. I wonder why she won't look me in the eye. I wonder if she remembers the pretend cigarettes and booze.
    She doesn't talk. I talk too much.

When I bled for the first time on New Year's Day of 1999, my parents threw a party. We drove from Boston to Canada and hired out a reception hall that specialized in Hindu celebrations. *Mangal neeratu vizha* loses its poetry when it spells "puberty ceremony" in English.
    My parents hired a makeup lady who pulled and tugged my unruly hair into a bun, put in extensions so that my hair hung down in a flowered braid and ended at my butt. My chubby body was wrestled into a saree. The blouse was tight and I could barely breathe. The makeup lady pinned jewelry to my head and brushed powder on my face, and when she was done, there was someone pretty looking back at me from the mirror. As a last touch she pressed a fake nose ring into my septum. It was jeweled and dangled in front of my mouth. All day long I suppressed violent urges to sneeze.

I watch my mother kill mice. I kneel on an office chair, pumped up to its full height so I can see the frigid steel of the lab table from my fourth grade height. The mice are a white that matches my mother's lab coat. She pulls them one by one out of their cage labeled "Test Group Four." They have to die, she says, because they are sick.
    She presses a black sharpie to their necks and they are dead, just like that, with little *tuk* sounds.

INSIDE THE V.A. DICTAPHONE TYPING UNIT, DIVISION OF OUTPATIENT PSYCHIATRY, 1969 – MARIA TERRONE

I felt like a voyeur at my gray steel desk,
wired from ear to tape recorder, recorder to foot,
bound to the veterans of Vietnam who confessed
to night sweats, panic, drunken bouts, brute
scenes erupting in their stricken minds
like bomb-blasted earth. Their words bored
through my ears all day and spread inside
me, shrapnel that tore at the heart of a girl
who hadn't yet known sorrow, men or war.
When I couldn't hear them, I pumped a pedal,
retreading the same scorched ground. The force
of demons propelled some voices--fierce as metal,
urgent as sex. But some whispered, and I saw faces
pain-twisted, men still pinned to a ravaged place.

THE JUMPER – CHRISTIN GEALL

I spotted him like you might a bird through the top of a windshield; a man perched on the rail of an overpass. An easy target. Or at least easier to hit than my car doing eighty, if you stop to think about the weight of a man, that specific correlation between velocity and mass. Measure that weight of probability, and if he'd aimed right, tried harder, thought longer, even practiced on a grassy verge before he'd jumped...

I'd have killed him.

You see: I knew the instant I saw him up there that the bridge wasn't high enough; he needed a car. He needed someone else to do it for him.

Before he jumped, there was just a green overpass on highway 295, between Yarmouth and Freeport, Maine. It was a quiet Sunday morning in the northbound lane and I drank drive-thru coffee en route to an alumni meeting, housed in a stone mansion up the coast. I'd come from British Columbia, out of loyalty, which pulled me back, two years after graduation, to that familiar highway, to the air heavy with humidity, the scent of summer salt marsh and low tide.

Then, I saw him. Lit up by the sun, his body faced south. He wore clean chinos, a forest green shirt that I remember tucked in, even with two arms slicing at the air his shirt stayed belted at the waist.

What do you do with that?

Push your foot on the gas and swear into the empty space of the car: *You f'ing bastard.*

I could explain myself this way: my mother killed herself like this, but she did it effectively, in a dirty Toronto subway tunnel, a hundred or so feet out of the College Street station. She walked down the tracks. Maybe sat patiently, waited cross-legged or leapt out from a blackened wall in front of an accelerating car. There was a driver, and headlights on the train. So my family sent flowers to that driver. And I never stopped to think about that fact. Never thought to think what it would be like to have killed someone, to be implicated and scarred by their choice, and the last image of them, until the jumper came towards the roof of my car. It seemed like selfishness, then, purely defined, an etching burnt forever on the memory of one person by someone who chose to leave memory behind.

The jumper landed on the pavement in my rear-view mirror, a low bump in the shadow of the overpass twenty feet behind my car. On a slow-motion reel of swerving vehicles, I counted three cars and one tractor-trailer truck behind me. He got to his feet, swayed, stumbled to the side of the road and vanished as the highway curved out of sight.

Perhaps the body remembers first, instinctively. I swore, and swore and drove and swore and I did not stop, did not pull over or get out of the car, did not even reach for my cell phone to call the police. I drove fast, away, up an empty highway, just as I'd survived at eighteen by not looking back, by leaving Toronto and its memories behind me.

The jumper landed in my life twenty years after my mother's suicide. For those twenty years I've missed her like a person might miss a foot; my own attempt at motherhood and creating a family, a clumsy, staggering success. Over that time, I've not judged my mother much, never borne more than a twinge of teenage guilt for her depression. I've sought instead to understand the reasons behind her dark journey towards Younge Street that day, sought to write my way towards answers to the questions that I can't ask her. I took a young woman's route towards and around grief, a path that didn't lead me to anger.

Nearing the stone house, I assembled myself, then chastised myself for not stopping. Others would have asked the jumper: *Are you alright?* Leant over him. Rested a compassionate hand on his back and looked into his eyes. But I couldn't do that. My actions weren't those of a caring citizen or even those of the mature woman I thought I'd become. I'd found myself a teenaged daughter, in flight, enraged. The only question I'd have had for the jumper was one I'd never asked of my mother: *How the hell could you do this to me?*

No one was hurt, I later found out. A few cars hit the guardrail, but everyone, it could be said, walked away unharmed. The northbound lane closed for a while, and then the Sunday traffic resumed as people headed down east for vacation. Back on the highway after my meeting, I noticed the tide had turned as I drove south. Near Yarmouth, under the bridges, the marshes had filled with seawater. Maine sailed by my windows, the afternoon heat shimmering the road ahead. I leaned my head over the steering wheel to look up at the overpass maybe thirty feet above me. All I could see was a light sky, the kind you'd expect after a storm.

PASSING THE CUPS – ELAINE NEIL ORR

She reads that when Western culture starts showing off the bosom, some catastrophic event is being heralded: the onset of war or economic recession or political upheaval. The signs aren't good. Her female students' breasts are swelling. Surely, she thinks, eyeing young women in her university classroom, those are not your natural size and so thrust up. Have you heard of gravity? She wonders if she says it out loud.

Not only are the breasts uncommonly large but the clothing has shrunk. What are parents thinking, the ones paying for their daughter's augmentations and their wardrobes? They might contribute instead to a summer abroad or a writing workshop or a kayak. What an odd contrast with the parent who wished—not long ago—to shield his daughter. As if super-sizing your offspring's breasts is something you would want like a Humvee or some investment against the future.

She remembers a gentle comment by a teacher when she was twelve, a reminder to use deodorant, and how ashamed she had felt to learn her body's fault. What in the world does it mean to a girl that her parents approve an entire overhaul?

She tries not to look but it's hard. She wants to know how many are surgical and how many owe their pomp to a wonder bra. None, it seems, slopes gently down before rising to the peak of the nipple, like a ski slope. Such breasts as that show their weight. No. These are all round grapefruits; the sense of flesh, gone.

At a coffeehouse across the street from campus, she notices a woman in a pea green sweater whose breasts are so large and so uniform and so, well, high, that she understands for the first time why some men refer to breasts as a rack. This woman's chest might have displayed earthenware crockery.

She attends a lecture by a poet interviewing for a job in her department. The woman displays her cleavage. Throughout the candidate's talk, her eyes are fixed on the woman's chest and when she sits beside her at dinner, her gaze is drawn over and over right there, to that alluring tunnel, like a secret path in a garden, leading to some rich grove. After the interview, she considers the likeliness of taking the same approach to job hunting. She never has. The reason seems obvious. In size, her breasts fill demi cups.

Yet she has never wanted larger ones. Smaller hips, yes, but not larger breasts.

Until her own began to show, she had received mixed lessons in breasts. Some of these came in the company of her elder sister and girl friends. She remembers entering the shadowed bedroom of someone's mother. They stand before a chest of drawers. The second drawer is opened. In it are light-foam pads. They take turns placing two of them under their cotton shirts and observing the effects. She is probably four years old. She remembers no conversation, only the ritual of passing the cups. Then they replace the foam objects in the drawer, close it silently, and leave the room. The entire episode evokes the feeling of something or someone already dead. Later, probably in the same year, she and her sister attend a pajama-party with older girls; again she is the youngest. What she most remembers is whisperings about stealing someone's bra, soaking it in water, and putting it in the freezer. All of the action takes place on a plane high above her. They sleep little and by the following morning she is so disoriented, she wishes never to endure this quality of entertainment again.

Her family lives in Nigeria; her parents are missionaries. Like her sister and herself, the other girls are white American daughters. For her the cold brassiere and artificial forms seem hugely at odds with the full warm hours of her everyday life. In that life, the British Empire has not succeeded in colonizing the African fashion world. She sees hundreds and thousands of Nigerian women who wear no bras and no blouses, whose breasts are as exposed as her elbows. There is great variety in breasts but in every case the skin of breast and chest and arm and leg is uniform in tone and color and in this way different from her mother's breasts, which are whiter than the rest of her, with the areoles the shade of a pink-lavender crayon. This whiteness and the pink-lavender centers seem the cause of the hiding and also the source of a shame. For the girl, brassieres become a necessary form of shelter for a vulnerability she will one day inherit. That future life will require more time indoors than out and all kinds of hooks and eyes buttoning up. She shuts her mind against the thought. Only much later will she be able to imagine how her young parents might have been challenged in their own domestic arrangements by the presence of all of those breasts, even among their congregants, how her mother may have felt herself exposed in spite of her clothing and perhaps even because of it. In her own continuum, the girl is nine when she glimpses, on a rare visit to the U.S., her grandmother's corset and built-in brassiere hung on the bedroom door. It looks like the skeletal remains of some oceanic creature, a fearsome sign of the life and death awaiting her.

She gravitates toward books full of fairies and water-babies and Peter Pan, hardly any girls, no women. These characters are neither male nor female. They're simply human. She imagines herself some cross between Peter Pan and Tinkerbelle. She and they are all light and pastel and flat-chested.

Her breasts begin to grow about the time faint hairs appear on the smooth plane of skin between her legs. She calls her mother into the bath, where she is soaking, head back, spread eagle in the tub, pretending at least that it is a swimming pool. Her natural habitat is a cold river in a hot climate where you bathe of an afternoon but this is the year of discovering Grandmother's corset and she is in South Carolina in a ceramic pond in a small brick house on a square lawn. Her mother has little to say that can reassure the girl and she feels sullied if not ruined. It must be that her mother shops for training bras because she has them ready for her a few months later, back in Nigeria, when the girl is packing for boarding school in a nearby town. But the bras find little purchase on her chest, slipping up every time she raises her hand in class. She tosses the new underwear onto the floor of her closet where gecko lizards nestle and goes back to wearing an undershirt. Eventually she grows enough to fill an A cup, though unfortunately the bras her mother now provides are conical—she must have found them at a British/Nigerian department store—and the tips are never full. She tries stuffing them with Kleenex but still they crumple beneath her thin dresses. She believes her breasts are not finished. They look a little abrupt, a beginning, not an ending. Surely they will get to B, she thinks. With friends at night in the dormitory, she engages in exercises meant to improve the bust line. Her chief rival, a dark-haired beauty with a small bottom and a finely chiseled face, enjoys fulsome breasts and popularity. She envies her, though it isn't her breasts she wants but her calm assurance of desirability. She doesn't yet understand the logarithm of women's breasts and male attraction and it's just as well she doesn't. By the time her sixteenth year has come and gone, it is clear she is destined for a life of 36A. She will never, like her mother, bend forward to land her breasts, nipple first, in the cups, a kind of aerial maneuver she had expected some day to master.

But smaller breasts have advantages. They don't hurt when she runs or get in the way of sleeping on her stomach. Hers are dainty and precise. They fit nicely with her inherited sense of tact and gentility. And they do little to disturb an intense identification with her father she has cherished and embellished since infancy. She intuits that her breasts befit her very being, as her name does, as does the gait of her walk.

She like her father is tall and athletic. Their long legs make them agile and blessed, like the winged creatures of her girlhood fantasy. She does not want to line up with her mother anyway, nor her sister, both of whom are clumsy and large-breasted. They sit and talk, clearly fated to a life of mere earth-walking. As far as she is concerned, high-flown rhetoric never lifts her mother one inch off the divan. But remembering that white vulnerability, the corseted but nonetheless all-too-present show of her mother, she feels sorrow and sometimes kisses her impulsively before leaving the house. She promises herself she will one day make it up to her, this abandonment.

In American magazines that make their way into her African school like capsules from another planet, she finds an angle of support. Large breasted Liz Taylor is passé. She doesn't even know who Elizabeth Taylor is but she can tell by the lipstick and arched brows and a desperation that lingers in the woman's eyes that she is lost. In all of the photographs of the once-envied beauty, the photographer is above her looking down. Not so with the coterie of new long-legged models in short skirts, all of whom look thin and flat. Like giraffes, they occupy the sky, the angle of the photo ever upward.

She might have been confused by glossy advertisements for brassieres that filled the same magazines had they not been so bizarre she read them as cartoons. In the stories of these ads, women are being urged to dream of where they might go in a Maidenform bra. Some options are riding a roller coaster and square-dancing. A woman could even dream of being sawed in half in her Maidenform. Another advertisement promises a brassiere to lift and separate, but separate from what? The language seems oddly technical and ominous, the object of that verb so ambiguous.

So she is not disappointed. Her smaller breasts seem just right. She probably loves them. They are lockets that don't open. Their secrets are hers and the secret is that they are hers. She has all of her life wished for a demure smile, a quiet, mysterious aura. She has wished for this providence because in general and in spite of her good breeding in precision and gentility, she is often brash and out-spoken and any stranger can read her face. Her breasts become her soft, sealed lips, her private Mona Lisa.

She is joyous, really, in her image, and ponders the muscle of her heart, its tremendous quiet rhythm, and how it beats for her.

PHONE CALL TO DUBLIN – KERRI FRENCH

I was in Galway with a group of girls
I no longer like. It was a bank holiday weekend,

3 a.m. on the first night. Our hostel was dirty
but cheap, so we laughed off the peels of wallpaper

over drinks, stumbled to our beds in the dark.
I awoke to a man already on top of me,

his hands holding down my arms, the weight
of his body flooding the space between us.

It took 21 seconds for my mouth to remember
how to scream. Afterwards, the pattern on the walls

shook in small circles as I dialed your number,
wanting nothing else in this country but your voice.

If I were to tell someone the first moment when
I knew I loved you, it would go like this.

ONTOLOGY – NANCY J. NORDENSON

Two palms, his and mine, pressed flat against the cool stone, newly tidied, a box buried below. I wonder now and always about this child who was never a child, but who may already see what no eye imagines, acquiring that full knowledge of what's really going on here in one fell swoop without having to so much as scrape a knee in search of it. Between visits, the ground encroaches. My husband scrapes the stone with a plastic card from a roadside assistance service pulled from the car's glove compartment, sliding it into the engraved lettering to free her name and epitaph, free the rosebud I had drawn once as instruction on gridded paper alongside "A time to mourn, a time to dance." My hand, its underside blackening, moves across the granite, pulling grass and sweeping dirt. We did the same at our last visit, and the one before that, and before and before and before. On snow we stood at this plot an age ago and placed grief next to hope in the company of pastor, family, and friends. Be still my soul sung in harmony. Pink flowers arrived and my milk came in and tears. Tears. For the price of a prom dress we bought that piece of land under weeping willows and old oaks. Smack in the middle of a brilliantly bright winter day the sales rep with his map led us through knee-deep snow. Two brothers waited. Why do people rush around so, I thought while looking out the car window at shoppers on the sidewalk as we drove home from the hospital with nothing but a bag of groceries in the back seat. When it was finished and I had left the room, I saw the green leaf cupping a drop of rain, a picture stuck on the doorframe, a secret code for the maternity floor staff: Don't ask to see a baby. Her head, hairless. On her forehead ordained fingers dipped in a vial of water drew a cross. In the name of the Father and the Son and the Holy Spirit, outside of time, inside of grace, I baptize you. The bundle stilled the world. Perfectly formed and wrapped in a blanket the nurse placed her in my arms. She had slid out, finally, not making a fuss and that was that. My husband told me, You're pushing her into God's arms. Where was the strength? The contractions fierce, fueled by the pitocin's drip, drip, drip. The body entombed on the ultrasound screen, bobbing not moving, like a waterlogged mango, had confirmed the worst, and so we began. The way there was too fast. Kick, baby, Kick! The exit is up ahead, and I can turn around, go home. I'd laugh later, that nervous laugh of danger evaded, but in the doctor's office it was hard to swallow. Telephoning my husband and sister to tell them where I must go, I nearly wept at the comfort of a hand laid on my shoulder, but when I turned no one was there. I held death but didn't know it. They did. So awkward they were at the silence in my belly. I lay on the table, cool crackly paper over black vinyl, and stared at the ceiling. These babies can get themselves in the strangest positions, they said, trying to smile. Slide the probe on its jelly lake farther to the right, no farther, now back, to the left, now up, and all will be well. How cheery, the midwife said when I arrived for the routine check. My new pink and green striped shirt was stretchy enough to last the months ahead. We were halfway. Not long before, an ultrasound showed in undeniable black and white everything anyone dares hope for: ten fingers and toes, lengths and circumferences in correct ratios, all organs present, a thumb being sucked. A heart beating. When exactly did it stop? I pulled a glass from sudsy water; I swept hair from my forehead; I blinked. Which of these moments was it, and why didn't it make itself known like a midnight strike at a century's turn? Of all the things to someday know, when blindness becomes sight and the last tear is wiped, I'll ask this first. My belly measured bigger than the month before, and the month before that, and a lifetime before, when my stomach was flat and smooth. His hand slid across my skin. Our lips touched.

TWO MOTHERS – CHAVAWN KELLEY

I thought if I loved myself and my child's father and the world we shared, the shallow alpine lake with a crust of ice around its edge, the poems of Rilke and the lilt of Claire de Lune, our child would come. Parents who lose a child grieve and their grief has a name. Their loss has a face and hair the color of wheat or sandstone, tree bark or a blackbird's wing. They may wear their grief to the store and others may view their sorrow.

But for the never-mother, hope may turn to grief when the injected fluid spills from between her thighs onto the paper of the radiologist's table and she lies in a pool of white dye and wet, unanswered whys. No car crash or fever or body of water takes her child. Only a gray dimming of hope. And as that child of my husband's and mine failed to take, I, too, began to dim, and the life, the very world I wished to share, slipped from me as well.

So how was it that this girl could be the one to restore myself to me? She didn't do it for me. She read the letter we wrote to someone unknown and unprepared to raise the child of her pregnancy. She read about us, our life, our pets, our house, our great desire. Later, we learned that she read more than a hundred letters. Ours, she said, was one of the few that didn't dwell on the magnitude of the baby's room. We wrote about each other, my husband's music, my garden, and the backcountry etiquette of leaving a campsite clean. She chose us. And each day within her, her baby grew.

Before he was born, her family gave us a present, a fleecy penguin suit with little feet. And on the card, she wrote, "You'll never be alone again!" I think she meant that as a single mother, she never had a moment to herself. But I'd had plenty, and for me, it meant I'd never be alone in the old way again.

She handed Joseph through our tears into my arms.

"Tell him I love him," she said. "Tell him it's not because I don't love him."

My husband and I fumbled through new parenting, one day after the next, until on the third night, Joseph began to cry and wouldn't stop. A diaper change made the crying worse. He would not take formula. He would not be comforted by holding or by massage to his tummy or his back. I understood then the absolute helplessness, the shot nerves, of the frantic mother. Joseph's cries were loud and sustained. We took turns, but after two o'clock, Shaun had to say, I'm sorry, and he went to bed.

That night, I felt if I did not do this right, if we didn't get through, she would get a call from the agency. See, we weren't deserving after all. But there was something else too. Let him buck. I could do this. I could outlast this red-faced screaming boy, just as she must have held her first child, alone, crying, after he was born. You just cry, little one. I can hold you here and rock you in the dark longer than you can cry. And I did.

I had a friend once who, when he was young, sat in front of the television expecting to hear on the evening news that his sister's baby had been born. The village bells *should* ring! They rang for us when we got home. So I remember being startled upon seeing a mother pushing a stroller with a baby newer than our own. I came close to tears the first time I packed away the baby clothes he had outgrown. But in an age-old way, newborn excitement eased into month-by-month development. Dr. Sears wrote in *The Baby Book* that the second nine months are as important as the first. I didn't believe him, but I was glad when the umbilical cord fell off and our history with our son began to accrue.

This is what I want to say: She was reckless and I was safe. I ate vegetables. She ate meat. She was brave and I hung on. My son is her son and she is his shadow mother—she is missing one. I'll always miss not carrying a life, part the man I love, part me, part ancestors of us both. My son carries her genes. And she is part of me. She and I are Joseph's mother, and in that, we are one.

SILOZI SONG – JILL N. KANDEL

She sat before them, uncomfortable, a baby in her arms. It was new and barely dry, less than twenty-four hours old. She was hot; the baby fussed and smacked.

They sat before her, black-eyed and heavy-breasted, in their best though tattered dresses with stained and reeking armpits. A formal delegation they sat, their wide and crack-soled feet waited, motionless. A toddler squatted in the corner of the room and the warm odor of pee wafted as a yellow puddle spread across her cement floor.

Her baby cried and would not still. Before the dark and silent eyes she tried to nurse the babe she barely knew, fumbled, tried again. The newborn needed only a second chance.

"Aiee, you will be good mother," the old one said to her and nodded singsong style.

She knew some of them, Anna, Inunge, Mrs. Biemba, and Patience. The others she wasn't sure. They asked her many questions and she tried to concentrate as the sweat ran down her back, puddled on the cracked vinyl chair, and seeped into yesterday's stitches. And the baby pulled and cried.

She didn't know what to say and tried to make a joke. "I'm glad the electricity was working. I'd still be in there pushing if it wasn't for the suction pump."

The old one nodded and laughed knowingly while everyone joined in. The children felt the laughter and began to dance at their mothers' knees.

They drank orange Sunquick quietly from plastic cups. The children spilled on the floor—sweet orange mixed with stinking yellow already there—and climbed sticky footed into their mothers' laps.

The old one came and picked up the baby. Tender like a grandmother, with wonder. She spoke quietly into the baby's ear. Softly in SiLozi she whispered. Her deformed hand placed a coin into the tiny perfect palm and then she gave her to another.

The girl child, the firstborn, was passed around the living room. Each mother held her and pressed an ngwee into her hand until it was filled with dirty copper coins, each one worth less than a single penny. Each mother held the newborn and blew a SiLozi song into her life.

May you never be in want.

May you never be without.

And the Zambia born child slept silently, unaware of the new language in her ear, while the old one stood to talk.

"You have done great thing," the old one said. "You, you bring new person in this world. Today we honor to give you new name."

She listened as the old woman spoke. A new name? She had lived for two years under the African sun on this edge of the Kalahari Desert. Lived with her Dutch husband who spoke only of crops and seed and soil. Lived in this sandy, snaky village, a twelve hour canoe trip separating her from the nearest town. She had lived here for two years and had never had her own name. People called her Mrs. or Miss. Mostly she was called by her husband's name: Mrs. Johan.

The old woman continued, "We Lozi, we call woman by name of firstborn. We call you Mother of Melinda."

"And if I have another child, will you change my name again?" she asked.

The old one laughed. "No, Mother of Melinda. This will not change. This baby is firstborn. You are woman, true."

The room fell silent. Then Anna spoke the question on everybody's mind.

"Mother of Melinda, why did you shaved her head?"

"What?"

"What meaning to shave her hair?"

"I didn't shave her head. White babies are born bald. Well, some are born with hair and some aren't."

Born a full month early her child had no hair, neither eyelash nor eyebrow.

"It will grow," she said defensively, but Zambian babies were born with full heads of hair and all the eyes looking at her did not believe. She knew these women saw her baby ever bald and she could not explain.

There were many things and happenings that she could not explain. She stayed there four more years. She had a son. Six years worth of her life she lived in a land so far away that it does not exist.

But still she thinks of those women who came and blessed her child. Those women who gave her a name when she had none.

She wishes they could see Melinda now, her hair plush in amber waves. She wishes she could see the women again, but she cannot. Most of them have died, and most of that dying from AIDS.

But every morning, of every day, she remembers.

And she knows her name.

WHERE DO BABIES COME FROM – JENNIFER BRENNOCK

I don't like the color of my nipples. They're too pale. They've never been permanently rouged by the chore of mother's milk. They remind me of what I'll never be and make me fear the question: Mommy, where do babies come from?

I dread my son's inquiry not because his adoption is a secret or a shame. My son already knows the words birthmom, forever family, and foster. What he doesn't know yet is this is unusual, this is not the way it goes for all babies, and when I tell him babies grow in their mother's womb, he'll know I didn't turn my body inside out for him. He'll know I'm only proxy; I am not real.

It's a chilly morning. He wants to climb in the big bed. I pull the down back around us. He wraps the end of his white blankie around his fist like the bandages of a boxer preparing for a fight. He inserts double fingers into his maw and sucks. I nuzzle him inhaling his morning odor. I put his feet between my knees to warm them. I pat the fuzzy bottom of the one-piece jammies he'll soon outgrow.

"Don't 'fmell me, Mommy. Pet."

He picks up my hand and puts it on top of his head. I begin the routine. I smooth the hair from his temple as slowly as I possibly can and repeat. His eyes close. They'll open when I stop. I remember the double spin his hair makes in the back, two spirals of fine dark hair spinning in opposite directions, evidence of his intensity. I wonder if she noticed, his real mother, his double crown on the day he was born. I remember his belly button is a spiral too and smile. This one I don't have to share with her. She didn't stay with him long enough to see the umbilical nub, the last bit of her body's link to his, shrink over days and fall off in the bath.

In the bed, he says, "Mommy, can we watch Scarlet's Web?"

"Not right now, Baby," I whisper.

He squirms and rolls toward me.

"Let's pretend Scarlet's Web. I'm the baby pig and you're the mommy pig and I feed you." He yanks the t-shirt I'm wearing to my neck as if to latch on.

"No, no, Honey."

I pull my shirt down and I'm suddenly filled with disappointment. I want to say "Yes, Honeypie" and put my nipple in his mouth, to flinch at the strength of it, to hold his head at the back of his neck and coo down at him while he takes what he needs from me.

Instead I tell my four year-old the mommy feeds the baby. All mommies feed their babies and is he hungry yet? I'll make him some oatmeal. I'll write his name in it with syrup the way he likes it.

It's years before and I'm reading a book about becoming an adoptive mother when the phone rings—the state. I hold the receiver while it buzzes. For a moment the tiny screen of caller id looks like the first ultrasound print-out that couples gleefully stick to their refrigerators and cubicles and fit so nicely in the custom pocket that the baby books all have now.

When I finally pick up, my kind adoption worker tells me we're up for another selection committee next week. "Have you finished the book yet?" she asks. It's still in my other hand—*The Primal Wound*. I've just finished a chapter that told me the child I adopt will never really love me if he doesn't grieve the loss of his real mother. The book says I have to teach him how to do this mourning, to initiate his grief. I remember the NPR feature about adoptees that made me pull over on the side of the highway. It said if he holds eye contact with me for a count of ten without looking away I will know he loves me, only then will I know I am real.

"Another committee? Which one?" I ask.

"I can't pronounce his name," she says. "I'll just give you his number."

I write the case number down and stare at it. I wonder if I can learn how to pronounce a number.

My morning child is eating the oatmeal quickly. It's joyous to watch him eat. We've taken the breakfast outside. The water sounds like secret laughter and the chaos of a flock overhead makes us both look skyward. He reports the news.

"Teacher has a baby growing in her belly and it's going to come out in a hospital and grow up tall and play soccer just like me," he says looking at the birds.

"How exciting. Maybe your teacher will feed the baby when he's hungry just like the mommy pig does on Charlotte's Web? Think so?"

His eyes meet mine now. A reflex, I start counting to ten. His eyes are suddenly passionate. I prepare for the question. I steel myself. I'm as ready as I'll ever be. *Out with it*, I silently plead. My count is at four.

"Mommy?" He asks wiping oatmeal from his chin, relocating it on his cheek.

"Yes?"

"Mommy."

Five.

"What, Honey?"

"Mommy?"

Six. I'm so nervous I'm sweating.

"Mommy?"

Seven.

"Just ask me, Honey. It's okay, Buddy, you can ask me anything."

Eight. Oatmeal falls off his spoon to the grass.

"Mommy, I'm not going to wash my hair tonight!"

At nine, he looks away and shoves an empty spoon into his mouth with defiance.

I laugh. "Let's see what happens."

"My rocket is going to grow a baby too."

As I listen to the details of rocket gestation, I nod and watch the sky. Clouds above are joined and undone in mere seconds. I've been given a reprieve and I am so grateful for it. For at least one more day, perhaps the very last one, I'm allowed to remain real.

RUMOR HAD IT – DILRUBA AHMED

she jogged the river trail
        in a sari. Chiffon layers

draping crooked arms,
        atchel whipping

in the wind. White
        running shoes pounding

along the Hocking.
        She blurred

into a mad red
        bird. Through screened

windows I heard a flurry
        of silk or slapping

soles—tried to catch
        a flash of damp

tendrils at her neck. Faceless
        she flew

over houses and fields
        while I searched the sky

for her sweat-soaked sari, longed
        for a glimpse

of her unraveling bun.

IRAQ 2003: GETTING BOMBED – KELLY HAYES-RAITT

Iraq taught me to drink.

Not while I was there, of course, interviewing women on the verge of war just five weeks before this recent US invasion. In a move to appease religious fundamentalists, Saddam Hussein had banned drinking in restaurants, bars, hotels and other public places, driving drinking behind closed doors and driving prices beyond the reach of most sanction-poor Iraqis.

It wasn't until I got home, safely cocooned in my tight living room in Los Angeles, watching CNN's incessant "shock and awe" war coverage while meticulously, relentlessly scrapbooking photos of Iraqis I met who might, at that very moment, be getting bombed, that I got bombed.

Night after night. Religiously. "Please go home and ask your president not to bomb us," the Iraqi women's pleas clung like meniscus in my wine glass. Every night, I prayed to numb my shame and helplessness and profound sadness... And every night I failed, finally passing out among the scattered images.

The numbers were too huge. Too impersonal. We dropped 90,000 tons of explosives on the entire country of Iraq during the 42 days of the 1991 Gulf War. On March 18, 2003, during the first day of bombing just Baghdad, we dropped *ten times* that amount. On people I'd met. Photographed. Befriended. Shared meals with. The numbers were impersonal, but the faces weren't as I memorialized them in my scrapbook.

We didn't bomb people at their best. In 1991, American bombs destroyed Iraqi roads, bridges, electrical grids, water and sewage treatment plants. Schools. Hospitals. Homes. Efforts to rebuild were crippled by government graft and by the United Nation's sanctions, which forbid the importation of spare parts – and of chlorine, which was suspected to be a component of chemical weapons. Iraqi attempts to rebuild their sewage treatment plants, for example, were futile. Consequently, 500,000 metric tons of raw sewage were dumped into the Tigris and Euphrates Rivers *daily*, contaminating downstream drinking water. In a country that had enjoyed top-notch health care in the 1980s, typhoid jumped from 2,000 cases each year to 27,000/year during the following decade and childhood diarrhea quadrupled to where the average Iraqi child had diarrhea 14 days a month, according to a January 2003 report by the United Nations called "Our Common Responsibility: The Impact of a New War on Iraqi Children." In less than a generation, health care deteriorated so precipitously every other family experienced the death of a child under the age of five.

And that was *before* this new war.

"The situation was not good before [this] war," explains Dr. Mohammed Masser, head pediatrician at the Basra Hospital for Obstetrics and Pediatrics, as he clicks his worry beads at a small group of us who had returned to Iraq a few months after the invasion. "Previously, there were no drugs, no sanitation, no electricity. I had one patient die every month because of cancer, but I [had] five people die every day from diarrhea due to malnutrition."

This new war crushed the overwhelmed public health system. To help Iraq cope, the *Croce Rossa Italiana* erected an emergency M*A*S*H-style tent hospital in a vacant parking lot next to the old prison in Baghdad. A series of connected tents housed hospital beds, gurneys, IVs, the pharmacy, the mess tent, creating a self-contained collapsible hospital behind barbed wire and nonstop gunfire.

During my follow-up trip three months after the initial invasion, Anna Prousse, a volunteer EMT from Milan, introduces me to Ebade, a fragile infant who had diarrhea for 49 consecutive days. "She came in more dead than alive," says Anna matter-of-factly. "She screams regularly now, so she will be OK."

The Italian volunteers distribute 8,000 plastic bags of filtered water each day to schools, orphanages and hospitals. This feels like a meager effort in this country whose 13 million children represent half its population and all of its future. Still, pediatricians at the bustling tent hospital treat between 150 and 180 Iraqi children every day who suffer from malnutrition, hepatitis, meningitis and typhoid, Anna explains, raising her voice over another round of nearby gunshots.

"We see everything," the detached professional says. I follow her gaze to the endless line of Iraqis waiting in the 120 degree afternoon heat to be seen by a doctor. "Thousands of children with desperate diseases, some we haven't seen before. Some are congenital – many families marry among themselves. Some of the congenital diseases are due to depleted uranium."

In 1991, the 320 tons of depleted uranium used to fortify American bullets – the nuclear waste that enabled our munitions to penetrate armor more efficiently – embedded in the soil, working its way into the food chain. Over the next decade, doctors would trace the areas where the depleted uranium had concentrated by tracking the increase in birth defects, still births and childhood leukemias. Compounding this environmental and public health time bomb, the UN estimates the US military used another 1,000 to 2,000 tons of the radioactive nuclear waste during this recent invasion.

"Most patients have come from areas with heavy bombing," says Dr. Mohammed Kamil, head of pediatric residents at the Basra Hospital for Obstetrics and Pediatrics, as he describes his young cancer patients. "The children with cancer – only one percent will live. We can't get the chemotherapy. We cannot tell people their children will die; we just do our best." Since depleted uranium has a half-life of 4.5 billion years, listless leukemia wards won't be any less crowded for decades to come.

Before the war, the women's peace delegation I traveled with toured the children's leukemia ward at Baghdad's Al Mansour Pediatric Teaching Hospital, visiting room after room after room of leukemia-stricken children and their weary mothers. Each room had four big hospital beds, made more gigantic by their diminutive patients tethered to IVs. Small cots and lockers next to each bed allowed the mothers to live at the hospital with their dying children.

Our delegation members moved from room to room, child to child, passing out balloons and taking photos. As I passed through one room, a mother startled me by grabbing my hand and feverishly pleading with me in Arabic. I called for the doctor: "This woman needs something, she needs something for her son."

"No," the doctor translated the woman's urgent message. "She says she has everything she needs. She just needs peace."

She just needs peace. She asked me for my peace button, and she pinned it on her black *abaya*, while Ahmed, her son, sat cross-legged on his bed, dying.

She just needs peace.

Back home, I found no peace in either the 24/7 broadcasts of smoke and chatter and horror, or in the American responses to the urgent talks I give.

"You owe us an apology!" a man nearly leapt from his seat following my presentation during a lunchtime Rotary Club meeting, where I was clearly bombing. "You came here to tell us both sides of the story, and you've told us only one side. Besides, we should go over there and just nuke all those Arabs; they're looting their own country and dancing in the streets when they kill Americans."

There was a smattering of indignant applause among the polite, tense group. I took a deep breath.

"You're right," I responded. "I have told you only one side of the story, because that's all I have. I'm not an Iraqi, or a dissident, or a soldier. I'm just a woman from Los Angeles who got on a plane and went to Baghdad, and these are the people I met," I gestured toward the blown-up photos of the faces of Iraqis who personified my talking points. Real people I'd met who might literally have been blown up at that very moment.

"But don't you think it's important we hear from all sides *before* we send our young men and women to war?" I asked. The man visibly relaxed as I felt the tension exhale from the room.

"Regarding your other comment," I was on a roll. "It wasn't too long ago that Angelinos were looting our own city. There are Americans who make me proud, and there are Americans who make me ashamed. I never want to be judged solely by those who make me ashamed. I ask you to reconsider your comment."

Surprisingly, he nodded and uncrossed his arms.

Emboldened by my disarmed Rotarians, I addressed more than 200 audiences between our March 2003 invasion of Baghdad and the November 2004 reelection of President Bush, from fifth graders learning about the pillars of Islam to Congresswomen learning about the impact of the war on Iraqi women. Indifferent audiences, emotional audiences, angry audiences, I absorbed them all, reliving my experiences two or three or four times a week.

I took this war personally. Usually over a drink. Or two or three or four, detaching myself by draining another cheap Chardonnay.

I just needed peace.

During that first trip, before the war, while peace was still possible, our translator was a 44-year-old Iraqi woman, who lives in Dallas with her Japanese husband. Amira Matsuda arranged for us to visit her mother, brothers and sisters in Hilla, near the biblical city of Babylon.

Babylon's walled fortress was built 22 centuries ago – a city straight out of my early catechism days, a city that until this moment seemed more mythical than real. The Tower of Babel, an ancient World Trade Center of sorts, was destroyed in 482 BC by a God wanting to exert his dominance over man's arrogance.

Fingering its weathered yellow bricks, walking its worn pathways, standing in the shadow of the blindingly blue gates of Ishtar, I realize that an errant American bomb missing Saddam Hussein's nearby palace could again reduce Babylon to rubble, this time by a country led by a man on a self-proclaimed crusade.

Amira's family, like most Iraqis I've met, is warm and welcoming, immediately ushering us into the dining room decked out with a meal lavish enough to feed twice our group. Two long banquet-style tables overflow with a feast of a dozen platters heaped with every possible permutation of vegetables and chicken over steaming beds of rice. Huge rolls line the perimeter of the table, interspersed with bottled water.

I feel honored and embarrassed: At the time of my pre-war visit, 16 million of the 26 million Iraqis rely solely on monthly government rations.

Even the richest of families must spend three-quarters of their income on basic food. In spite of these hardships, every Iraqi I meet is eager to feed me.

Amira has nine remaining siblings; a brother is still missing from the 1980s war with Iran, another brother died during the Gulf War. At first Amira, with her long, flowing hair and western cut jeans, appears as foreign as we are in contrast to her sisters in their long, flowing coats and scarved hair. But she clearly belongs here and flows easily into conversational routine as if she'd never left.

In the kitchen I bond with her sisters, not by cooking, but by dishwashing. Ascertaining that I am unmarried – and a darn good dishwasher to boot – Amira's sisters immediately set me up as a bride for their widowed brother.

I don't quite understand all the hilariously assertive gestures and enthusiastic, high-pitched "la-la-la-la-las," but I go along with what I hope is a joke. We're on war-time; we dispense with the flirting and courtship and move straight to the mock marriage ceremony. War-time or not, I refuse to forgo a wedding ring, and the ladies understand when I point in horror to my empty ring finger. One of Amira's sisters produces wedding *earrings*, straight from a J.C. Penney box.

My make-shift wedding takes place in the dining room. Fake roses adorned with birthday candles complete my trousseau. Another delegate steps up as wife number two, and our husband-to-be praises Allah for his impending good fortune. The entire family gets in on the act, clapping and clowning.

He speaks only Arabic; I speak only English. He pantomimes a proposal; I order him to peel my wedding apple. Sitting in this ancient fertile crescent, 1,400 years after the prophet Mohammed inhaled eternal life through the fragrance of an angel-sent apple just before he died, I share an apple with my new Iraqi "husband," hoping its enduring powers will protect him and this lovely, lively family.

The last time I saw him, he came to our hotel in Baghdad to bid us farewell. Still complaining about the lack of a wedding ring, I joke and laugh and try to postpone the inevitable. I tuck in his lapel a marigold one of our hotel waiters has given me, a shock of orange against his grim grey suit.

When the bombs started falling, I wasn't there. I listened live on National Public Radio from the safety of my car half a world away, clutching my steering wheel on Santa Monica Boulevard, while honking drivers angrily passed me, going about their self-important day.

Later, I waited anxiously for news of my new Babylonian family. In Texas, Amira initially heard that everyone is okay, shaken, scared, edgy, angry, but alive. Over months, we hear of the deaths. First, Amira's elderly mother died when she couldn't get her medication.

Then, I hear my "husband" has died. The strain of the constant gunfire, the never-ending fear, took its toll on his heart.

I eat an apple in his honor, and I pour myself another drink.

IF WOMEN RAN THE WORLD – ELLARAINE LOCKIE

Hankies with holes and dried snot
hung as public assistance signs tied to a fencepost
in front of the house that bordered the railroad tracks
If wind whipped them into tumbleweeds
notches carved in hobo shorthand in the wood
advertised the community service

My mother fried Spam in bacon grease
minutes after the 5:15 screeched to a halt
The whistle having dinner-belled need for food
as dependably as the knock on the door
She squeezed the pink slices between buttered bread
that folded into recycled waxed paper
And delivered it to the man wearing whiskers
and filthy clothes waiting by the fencepost

Back then I saw it as charity
Even though Dad wore the look he did
when Mom made him go to church
The same look probably that Grandpa wore
when Grandma made pork sandwiches for Roasting Stick
whenever he appeared on his horse
at the edge of their homestead

Grandpa said *Woman, those Indians are gonna scalp you*
She built a bartering business with the Cree anyway
Homemade lye soap and pickled pigs' feet
for chokecherries and peace of mind
Grandma knew how to hold onto her hair

In California I offer the plumber, tree trimmer
and furnace repairman
homemade cinnamon rolls and coffee
My husband wants to know why
since we're paying them

WOMEN WHO PAWN THEIR JEWELRY – SHEILA SQUILLANTE

They come after death, divorce or break-up
to sell jewels as bright and various
as their pain: topaz dangles for the ear, amethyst
bracelets, opal pendants, engagement
rings—each small decoration, each shiny icon
of promise, laid out on the counter,
tender to be redeemed.

Some are angry. They dump lengths
of chain in knots—*God damn him!*—in front of me:
tangles of unsolved computations. Here is a woman
in haste, who demands reparation. Who can blame her?
She never asked for perfection, only tenderness,
communication—maybe a back rub on her birthday,
someone to fix the occasional pot of tea.

These women—performers of foot massage and circus
acts of the bedroom—what can I say to them?
There is nothing. Their only consolation: a flat cash value.
I will go through the motions of appraisal: loop
to eye, facet by facet—that carbon-white wink
blinking back through jeweler's glass. It hardly matters
what I see, what flaws and discoloration in the body
of the gem: they will accept any offer—seventy-five,
one hundred dollars at most—and leave
me their gold for scrap.

MOOSE, LOOKING – ANNA LEAHY

It's the jowls, really,
and the water dropping from them,
the beautiful unslurping
just next to the car, idling.
And the brown
of its coat, molting,
and of its round eye
dark enough to contain the field, the ditch,
and the moose's large life.
And my life even.
The scene is unstartling
for the moose, and somehow
for me too
because of the jowls, the eye, and the slow
rise of its forequarters
from its hind
like the landscape itself
ambling up to me
for a long drink
I can never really have.

HAPPY BIRTHDAY – DINAH LENNEY

"Birthdays," says my mother, "they're boring. Useless. Who gives a shit about birthdays anyway?"

I'm calling her for good cheer but I should know better by now. I'm my mother calling to say I don't want to be older, I don't want to be in L.A., I don't want to be me! I'm hoping she'll say, *darling, you're a gem, don't be silly, you're beautiful and smart and everything will be all right*. Instead, she says, "Well, honey, I don't blame you. It's awful, isn't it?"

I'm an ass to call, an old dog to go in that direction for comfort. It was five years ago that my mother told me, regarding my looks, that I had about five good years left. It was just last summer that she mentioned, for the first time, that I should consider plastic surgery.

"I've noticed," she said, wiping her own eyes, all choked up, "I mean I only want the best for you, and I'm so afraid you'll bite my head off if I tell you what I think, but I love you, dear, and I've noticed, those bags under your eyes – if you were a teacher or a lawyer, I wouldn't say a word, dear, but after all, your work depends on your looks."

Since when? Since when did my work ever depend on my looks? I'm a character actress, understand, with respect to television and film, I was never the pretty one. I'm the neighbor, the best friend, the comic relief when I'm lucky; and otherwise, most notably (lucky me, since it keeps me in health insurance), Nurse Shirley on the medical drama *ER*," a kind of plot conveyer, actor as device, to move the scene along, as in: "You have a phone call, Dr. Benton," (and he takes it) or, "Here's your scalpel, Dr. Corday," (and she uses it), or, "Act like a man, Dr. Carter," (and he does).

To my mother I mumbled something about how I didn't really work all that much.

"But you want to," she asserted, "And if you want to, dear, you're going to have to get your eyes done." She blew her nose, put her hankie back in her big black satchel, snapped it closed.

Be your own *good parent*, said the shrink, years ago. Which means that instead of making an appointment with a plastic surgeon in Beverly Hills, I should look in the mirror and announce, "Hey, you look great! You've been waiting for this! Now you get to play the good parts! These are your salad days! Happy birthday to you!"

On Stage 11 one day at Warner Brothers, shmoozing in the operating room between takes, I ask one of the regulars, a beautiful woman a few years younger than I, if she'd ever consider plastic surgery.

"I don't know, I really don't. Would you?"

"These bags," I admit, "I'm wondering about these bags under my eyes…"

"Those?" she cries. "Those! I had those removed ages ago. That's not the same thing at all! They're not supposed to be there!"

What I should do is blow out the candles and get on with it. Instead, I call an old friend, a television star, and ask her who did her eyes. Then I drive to the West Side and spend three hundred dollars to hear that my mother is right: my eyes are puffy. Fat deposits, that's all. A simple procedure and no one will ever know. I'll look rested, relaxed, rejuvenated, like my, oh, say, thirty-five year old self. And hey listen, while they're at it, if I want they can suck a little fat from the top lids, too. Minimal bruising. Instant gratification. What? I thought the surgeon would tell me I was perfect and didn't need his services?

Five grand per eye, and if I do it within the year my three hundred dollars for the consultation works as a deposit towards the full amount. The receptionist takes my check and gives me a business card. She's preternaturally thin, a Gumby-like gazelle with huge unblinking blue eyes, practically lidless, perfectly polished nails and forty-plus year old knuckles.

I cry all the way home. Talk about puffy eyes.

When I was eleven, I cut off all my hair like Twiggy. My ears stuck straight out. My mother said, " Never mind, we can have them pinned back." The story goes that I was appalled; that I told her with more conviction than I've been able to muster since, they're *my* ears, I'll keep them the way they are.

Let me take a detour here to say it's my theory that we girls, at 11, are stronger, more powerful and more fully realized than we can hope to be again until after menopause. (Bring on those birthdays…) It's the menstruation thing, the hormones and all, that screws us up for forty odd years. Before and after, we have potential for magnificence.

When I was twenty-seven and fully a victim of my hormones, I went to an appointment with Bernie, a commercial casting director in New York City. Bernie looked at me, looked at my resume, looked back at me and said, "Can you do something about the wart above your upper lip?"

Think Cindy Crawford, think Madonna, think 1940s movie stars and a black sharpie, I just happen to have a mole, most aesthetically situated above my mouth, stage left of my nose, house right, if you're facing me head on.

"It's the food clients, see," said Bernie, "A wart right there, that close to the product, it makes them uneasy."

He scrutinized my face and peered hard at the offending spot, discomfiting, to say the least, when you're putting your best foot forward, trying to look a person in the eye and have a conversation. But clearly, Bernie wished to be helpful.

"You could cover it maybe?" he suggested. "With make up or something?"

"Well, Bernie," I explained, "it's in relief—that is, it's a *mole*, Bernie, it's a bump, make up can't touch it."

But for a week I wandered around the apartment with my index finger strategically placed to one side of my nose and just over the offending landmark. At the end of the week, contemplating cosmetic surgery for the *first* time, I asked my then boyfriend (now husband) for his opinion.

"How do I look?" I encouraged, "Be honest."

"You look," said Fred, "like a woman with her finger up her nose."

So now, I arrive home from Beverly Hills all puffy and distraught and announce that it will cost about ten grand to make me gorgeous again. A birthday gift from my mother, I add.

Fred blanches, then tells me I'm absurd. Our children go to public school. We've never taken them to Europe. We haven't saved a dime towards college or retirement and I am destined to get old like everybody else in the world. The deposit was three hundred dollars? Am I kidding? Am I crazy? Can I get it back? But then he takes pity on me and tells me I don't look a day over thirty-nine.

AFTER OVARIAN SURGERY – JENNIFER CHAPIS

She dines on blueberries in the bath.
Each slow berry a moment slipping.
Blue storm, rain-sounds. Her body is all steam,
velvet, snow—millions of minuscule air
bubbles cling, and wipe away like shaving
cream in thick stripes. Nothing holds the eyes

like the skin of a woman. Her gray eyes
shift from ceiling to bath.
She imagines a baker shaving
fur from a peach, fruit slips
from his knife, heart leaks like an air
mattress. The knot of him inside her. Steam

risen from a pastry, vanilla light. Its steamy
core silent, the hunter's lion eyes
its own rupture. Infinite. In mid-air.
I almost vanished. Red crawls about the bath.
Her insides are nothing, an itch. She slips
a bathing cap over her hair, and sinks. Seconds shave

by. *Breathe!* Petal-like soap shavings
slide over her thighs, pubis thick with steam,
and the incisions below the hips where a slip
might hang. Navel—a berry, eye
looking in. (Keep the incisions dry. Bathe
them in Bacitracin, vitamin E, let the air

nurse them.) She's near-met death before: in a hot air
balloon dragged by a shifting wind-stream—shaving
past a net of electrical wires. And in the bath
as a child. In this stolen porcelain dish, steam
sighs. It penetrates and undoes…. What owns the eyes
like this?—a woman dreaming, slipping

berries onto her tongue. Each one slips
furtively inside, her warmest self ajar. By air
and sea they travel the body. The berry an eye-
witness to the wants untouched. (Shave

the brain. Love the infant unconceived.) Oh, steamy berry, delicious sapphire, this jewel bath

red, blue—*My lion's heart slipped out, sunk and shaved. You are the air itself, and I a mother underwater.* Steam-opened morning glory, eye of this rich rich bath

YOU ARE I – JUDITH SLATER

One early Saturday morning in the spring of 1982, I drove two hours north from San Francisco to a commune my soon-to-be-ex-husband had joined. Keith and I were trying, not very successfully, to stay friends, and since the divorce had been my idea, I suppose I wanted to get a look at the place where he was living, to make sure he was all right. This sounds nobler than it was. I felt guilty about the break-up, though not guilty enough to change my mind, and I was always looking for reasons to make myself feel okay about it.

And Keith did seem genuinely enthusiastic about the commune, though he objected to that term. It was a research institute, he told me. Ukiah Research Institute. URI for short. URI members liked those initials. "You Are I," they wrote in the various pamphlets and newsletters Keith gave me to read. They shared everything – possessions, food, chores, money, sex. Of course sex.

I thought this might be just the place for Keith. He always had been an ideologue. Give him a topic like "the nature of evil" and a jug of wine and he could talk for hours. I admired that passion dimly, but mainly (it took me years to admit this) he bored me.

Keith had told me that Saturday mornings would be a good time to visit, because the group had its weekly meetings then. We had decided it would be best if Keith weren't there during my visit, since one of the bones of contention in our marriage was my need for more independence. I felt that whenever he was in the room, he overshadowed me. I had married him when I was barely twenty. Whatever was I thinking? Well, he was handsome; I was already friends with his younger sister; his mother was nice to me. Reasons enough. And then we were a couple ("You Are I"), and now I was thirty-one and it had become impossible to figure out who I was apart from him.

The people at the commune were expecting me. When I rang the doorbell of the ramshackle but comfortable-looking farmhouse, the woman who answered said, "You must be Judy. Come in." That was it for introductions. About twenty people sat in a circle on the living room floor. I can't remember what any of the men looked like, except for a blondish guy named Steve or Scott, who turned out to be the subject of much discussion that morning. The women were indistinguishable from one another, wearing bathrobes or baggy sweat pants, some of them wrapped in blankets because, although the morning was clear and bright, it was still early and a little chilly.

The meeting had already begun. No one paid any attention to me. I sat down on the floor, outside the circle. The rules of order seemed to be, basically, that each person in turn could talk for as long as they wanted without interruption. People usually started out with the phrase, "I notice." "I notice the sun coming in through the window." "I notice that my coffee mug is warm." "I notice that the air feels cold." The goal, apparently, was to be observant. Then the noticing got a little more pointed. "I notice that Scott" (or Steve – can't remember) "has been resisting our suggestions that he take more responsibility for keeping the house clean." "I notice that Scott or Steve has been missing a lot of our evening mealtimes lately." "I notice that Scott or Steve is very passive-aggressive." (Afterwards, when I asked Keith about this, he said that at each meeting, a different person was chosen to be talked about as though they weren't there. It was known as an "after the party" conversation – like when people talk about you after you leave a party, but in this case you haven't left. It encouraged honesty and self-awareness.)

There was also much talk about various books and essays on philosophy. Sometimes somebody would get so enthusiastic about an article he'd read that he'd leap up and go find it and then read it aloud to the group. An hour went by, and then another. My heart leapt when they got to the last person in the circle, but without even a pause, they started going around again. No one asked me to participate, which at first was a relief but then I began to feel a kind of bored panic. Was this never going to end? At one point, one of the women did "notice" me. "I notice Judy," she said when it was her turn, "and I wonder what she's thinking about all of this." She went on before I could decide whether I was supposed to respond. "And I notice that Scott or Steve has been really uncommunicative lately."

Keith and I had moved to San Francisco together a couple of years earlier, for no particular reason except the experience of it. I loved, instantly, the vibrancy of the city, so different from the sleepy Oregon lumber mill town where Keith and I had both grown up. I loved the smell of eucalyptus and the ocean. My favorite thing in the world was to get up early on a weekend and just walk. To Russian Hill, to Chinatown, to North Beach, stopping on the way to sit in coffee houses. Keith liked to sleep till noon on weekends, and by the time he was up and about, I'd already had a half-day's adventure on my own.

Keith didn't like the city; he missed the woods of the Pacific Northwest; he couldn't find a job he liked. He had always been sure of me. He admitted later that he'd always assumed that if one of us were ever to "outgrow the relationship," as he put it, it would be him. When he sensed me slipping away, he became scarily depressed. He slept even later, drank more, stayed up till four a.m. staring zombie-like at whatever happened to be on television. While I, seduced by the city, became more energized. I began to have flying dreams, where I floated out the bedroom window of our apartment and flew over the city in the dark, above all those glittering lights.

I already knew quite a bit about the commune from what Keith had told me. They had an elaborate system – not quite a schedule posted on the refrigerator, but almost – to ensure that every man would have sex with every woman (they were determinedly heterosexual – their sexual experimentation only went so far) on a regular basis; this was to avoid jealousy and possessiveness. However, a number of the members didn't really like each other, at least not enough to have sex. Also, they didn't call it sex, they called it "meeting," as in, "I'd like to meet with you." Or, "Tonight I'm going to meet with Scott. Or Steve." The sexual meetings were different from the Saturday morning group meetings, but looking around the room that day, I thought both kinds of meetings seemed equally dreary. Outside, the sun was shining. Why was everyone huddled inside unattractively, under blankets? Once in a while somebody would pad out to the kitchen and bring back a bowl of cereal, which they ate sitting on the floor.

At first I couldn't imagine just getting up and walking out – it would be awkward, rude – but as the hours went by I felt increasingly desperate. I don't think I'd realized till that morning the vast difference between Keith and me. If he'd been here, a talk like this would have energized and inspired him, whereas I was bored, literally, to tears. Finally, when one of the women got up to go into the kitchen (the same woman who'd "noticed" me and wondered what I was thinking), I followed her. "I'm going to leave now," I told her. She looked surprised. "Oh, okay," she said. Now that she was out from under the shapeless blanket, I saw that she was pretty, with long dark hair and dark eyes and a nice smile. Keith had slept with her. Met with her.

Someone was talking about Emerson's essay on the Oversoul when I walked out. Maybe one of them would say, "I notice Judy's left." Or maybe not. I left them to their earnest discussion, their odd rules of order. They were doing the same thing I was, after all, trying to figure out how to live, but they were doing it collectively while I was doing it alone.

As it turned out, URI wasn't the right place for Keith. He stayed there a year, maybe less, then either left of his own accord or was asked to leave (his explanation was fuzzy). Although he enjoyed all the discussion, all those ideas about how to build a better society, when it came right down to it he craved privacy. All that sharing, even of sex (maybe especially of sex), became oppressive.

I searched for URI on the internet recently, and found almost nothing, just one web site with a few reminiscences by a former member, who could even have been Keith, I suppose; the writer didn't identify himself. The group had disbanded a couple of years after Keith left, though it had probably lasted longer than most groups of its kind. The web site included some of the group's writings -- a raggedy manifesto with muddled lines like, "we are a group of people groping intuitively toward a more or less dimly shared vision for what is not only possible but intended by life," and, "...a social experiment designed to facilitate the realization of Cosmic Self."

The relief I felt when I left the place that Saturday was akin to those flying dreams when I floated up to the ceiling and out into the night, though not quite so easy or effortless. Driving down 101 towards San Francisco, all the windows open, I felt like some lumbering animal half flying, half lurching, towards freedom.

IF YOU KNEW – ELLEN BASS

What if you knew you'd be the last
to touch someone?
If you were taking tickets, for example,
at the theater, tearing them,
giving back the ragged stubs,
you might take care to touch that palm,
brush your fingertips
along the life line's crease.

When a man pulls his wheeled suitcase
too slowly through the airport, when
the car in front of me doesn't signal,
when the clerk at the pharmacy
won't say thank you, I don't remember
they're going to die.

A friend told me she'd been with her aunt.
They'd just had lunch and the waiter,
a young gay man with plum black eyes
joked as he served the coffee, kissed
her aunt's powdered cheek when they left.
Then they walked half a block and her aunt
dropped dead on the sidewalk.

How close does the dragon's spume
have to come? How wide does the crack
in heaven have to split?
What would people look like
if we could see them as they are,
soaked in honey, stung and swollen,
reckless, pinned against time?

NOT TOO OLD – MARGIE LUKAS

December is always cold in Nebraska, but that Friday afternoon was colder than most. With my grown daughters away, my son in high school, and my husband at work, I sat on the sofa alone. A book lay in my lap, but I couldn't read. I'd turned fifty in June and felt depressed and restless and wondered if my life had ever changed. I didn't resent my children for the years spent raising them, they were beautiful and compassionate, and I relished the memories of our late night talks and having always been there to greet them after school, but that book was closing. I had to face myself, and I felt as if I wore an invisible label, printed in smallish letters, Times New Roman font—no Edwardian Script or Curlz MT for me. The sign read: "Mediocre." One of fifteen children, I fell in the middle, and from birth I'd learned to occupy my middling roost in everything I did, even in how I thought of myself.

Was I experiencing a classic mid-life crisis? Or entering what author Jean Shinoda Bolen calls, "The Crone Age?" where women finally seek themselves? Either way, I knew nothing would change until I did. I'd reached the half-century mark and still no fairy godmother had come to tap pumpkins on my behalf. I needed to wield my own wand, and I determined to do so. Not by hurting those I loved, searching for a younger man or throwing away my heels for Birkenstocks to backpack across Europe. The change I sought wasn't in running away, but in finding the spirit I'd promised my children each of them possessed.

For years I'd dreamed of going to college—I'd not been in the thirty-three years since graduating from high school. Instead, I'd let every opposition, from every opinionated corner, thwart that dream. On that cold afternoon, with the wind chill hovering around zero, I decided this time I would not be stopped.

I called the admissions office at the local university and spoke to a nice woman who seemed interested in helping me enroll, but who informed me I couldn't start until the following fall. Spring classes would begin in just a couple of weeks and the processes of enrolling and acceptance were long. "August."

I couldn't wait; I was afraid to wait. Eight months of hearing how I was too old to handle the pressure, too old to mix with students less than half my age, too old to keep up with them academically—to say nothing of tuition costs—might stop me again. "Just tell me the first step I need to take."

She sighed. Listed ten.

A quote hangs over my desk (author unknown), which reads: "Go as far as you can and the Universe will meet you there."

I tried again. "What can I do *today?*"

Hearing the desperation in my voice softened hers, "You need your high school transcripts sent, and on Monday come and fill out admissions forms. But they will be for the fall."

I told her I was thirty minutes away, no, I was sorry, I couldn't wait for Monday. Before leaving, I called my high school, afraid my records from so long ago were lost or stored off-site in some cobwebby basement file. The secretary promised to put them in the mail yet that afternoon.

At the university, I turned in the forms, against the objections, requesting to start college that spring semester. Two weeks later I sat in an advisor's office looking for classes with still-open seating. Much to her surprise, but not mine, we found four classes that applied to my major. I wasn't surprised because everything thus far had fallen into place, and I felt as if the Universe were orchestrating events that matched my determination. The following Monday I walked into my first class.

Over the next four years, I found incredible people, students and faculty. I also discovered a world of new ideas. My house, my kids, my husband had been a neat, if insular, triad of focus.

In the spring of 2004, at fifty-four, I graduated summa cum laude. I wasn't really fifty-four though, going to school had taken thirty years off my mental and spiritual age.

I set my sights on graduate school and again met with a flood of objections. One professor assured me I'd be "wasting money even sending out applications. Graduate schools are looking for people with lists of publications, many applicants have already sold their first book." He didn't mention my age, that he kept in his mouth like a stone he struggled to talk around.

I'd already heard all the objections, and struggling through classes like algebra and biology had reinforced my belief that the only thing able to hold me back was self-doubt. Again, I'd do what I could and trust in the rest. I searched out graduate programs and because applications were expensive applied to three. ("Naïve," I was told. "One should always apply to at least ten.") The program I wanted most was a low residency program in Washington State, a region of the country I'd never visited. I was accepted.

The journey through college and graduate school had mountains and streams. Tuition, with a son in a private high school and still needing a college education, was a constant issue. The expense wasn't taking food off the table, but our bank account made an audible yelp with each payment. And for what? At my age, I wasn't going to find a tenure-track teaching position (not yet), wasn't going to spend forty years earning. By the time I finished the master's program, I'd be at the door of social security. Also, my degrees would be in writing: The profession of paupers.

I teach writing at that university now, I've published a couple of short stories, and my invisible sign reads "Stupendous." And maybe, just maybe, it's not all that invisible.

APOSTROPHE S – JENNIFER GIBSON

I
When Josie came to live with me,
she was fourteen months old.
An apostrophe-shaped slash on her chest.
The same chest my hands could span,
fingertips touching like an outside ribcage.
The wound took thirteen stitches.
Every day I traced the curve
with medicated cream
as it turned from blue to purple
then pink, raised and began
the long puckering into a thin line,
her eyes watchful as I dabbed and spread.
As she got older, she
sometimes still cried out,
in her sleep, in the bath,
in pain or fear or something more.
A miniature version in the mirror
of the woman she will become,
she studies her scar, fingers it,
questions its existence
less and less.

II
When Josie came to live with me,
I was four years out of gastric bypass,
a thin white line from breast bone
to belly button I showed off proudly.
I had gained mastery over my body,
made it endure
the side of a mountain, the seat of a horse.
Thirty years since it betrayed me,
since Poppy put his big hands on me. Now,
Josie's whole baby hand splayed out on one
ugly accordion-like flap of skin on my back,
leathery elephant fold on my stomach,
wadded up, smoothed out paper inner arm.
Her touch, just to get my attention

as I dressed. Skin to skin,
a feeling from so long ago.
I held my breath, waited,
allowed myself to become
the apostrophe
that replaces what's lost
and stitches us whole.

TRYING TO BE NORMAL – MARILYN BATES

It's Friday night. I'm all dressed up, out on the town, looking for a man. Sounds like something out of a 60's song, but the truth is, I'm still clinging to stereotypes, the "Guys'n Dolls" era, where women teetered on Lucite stilettos and men whistled at their swelled calves. At 50, I feel as though I've lost all my sexual prowess, adrift in a sea of perfect women with younger bodies and faces. No one knows that my feet are cramped inside a pair of "normal" looking Rockports, that the bottoms of them are as uneven as a rippled beach, mounds of bony projections like exposed driftwood. One of the side effects of diabetes is neuropathy or a numbing of the feet and hands, resulting in an inability to sense the floor normally. This causes one to smack the floor in such a way that the feet bones become inflamed and gradually "melt." It is a process of very slow, progressive deformity. I'm trying to conceal the fact that I maintain my balance by walking somewhat splay footed, pretending that my feet haven't been ship-wrecked by years of diabetes. If I wore these shoes more than a day at a time, I would rub a sore spot on my foot. Usually, I wear custom-made shoes that look like wooden clogs covered in leather--not the sultry espadrilles I once wore. I've nicknamed my unsightly shoes "clubble-humpers," an onomatopoeia for the sound they make on the floor. But I never wear them on social occasions where men are potential suitors.

I've already been to the restaurant where we'll all meet later. Its location is new to me, and unless I know my way there, I'll never be able to find it in the dark. I only see out of one eye now, the other ravaged by diabetic hemorrhage. The remaining eye is like an opaque window from a lighthouse trying to signal a ship in the dark. I'm not afraid, though, because my mind will remember where to turn in the road, even though I can't see the turn in the dark until I'm almost into it. This is what it takes, I keep telling myself, to be able to go out at night, have a "normal" life.

Dressing for the evening is an ordeal with numb fingertips, another aberration of diabetes. Putting on my jewelry is a nightmare. Holding the small lobster-claw catch out of sight behind my neck takes forever. Hooking it onto an open loop that I can't detect seems impossible. I can't feel my earring wire connect with the hole in my ear or sense the plackets on my slacks so that I can zip them up easily. Now I can't locate anything in my purse by feel--my keys, lipstick, coins, or a pen; all feel relatively alike.

At the party I'm trying to dissuade anyone from noticing my shoes by wearing tight slacks and a halter top with a spray of seed pearls covering the tip of a scar on my chest where I had open-heart, bypass surgery. The cleft between my breasts is matched by a dazzling south sea pearl I brought back from a cruise. The scar inside my leg--one doctors took the new veins from--is almost faded. Soon I can wear shorts again, but you can bet I'll keep my knees together, that is, if I want to appear perfect in a world where women outnumber men. Still, I can't help thinking I'm a fake because I'm limited as to how much walking I can do, and if I do manage a date, there'll be no strolls along a sunset beach, or hiking along a mountain trail, or rapid, high-heeled dancing. So why am I going to a singles' affair on a Friday night? I call it *not giving up*.

From the very beginning, my life has been about pretense, pretending when I was a young child of seven that the "rules" for diabetes didn't pertain to me--that I was above the caveats, the regimented diet, and if I defied the rules hard enough, somehow the side effects of my disease wouldn't eventuate. Now, I pretend that if I meet that one special guy, maybe he'll have a few health secrets, too, and that together we will form a relationship, and be more willing to "forgive" the other's physical shortcomings.

I venture into the singles' party, which is held at a marina filled with chatter, clinking bottles and glasses. Arnie, who I will soon meet, sits at the bar, confidently tilting a glass to his lips as he casually surveys the influx of single women. He appears to be my age, not especially good looking nor impeccably dressed, but he glances up from his glass and smiles at me. The singles group assembles at tables in the bar and, I make sure to sit near Arnie. He seems interested in my prattle.

I find that Arnie's wife died a year before, that he has a boat, likes guns, which immediately launches me into my desire to have an old gun cleaned and a chance at target practice, something I've been wanting to do. Arnie says he will have a look at my gun and take me to a target range sometime. I'm thrilled at this point.

He has a small security business, seems to know a great deal about listening devices and invasion of privacy, was in the military in a special security force, and is still in touch with some of the people he served with. I'm thinking that maybe he's a nut, suspecting the Government of listening in on our lives. I'll hang in unless he starts spouting UFO theory.

After dinner our group plans to meet at someone's house to schedule a charitable event. He asks for my number and writes it down on a napkin, then asks if I would like a ride on his boat moored at the dock. I love the idea of the boat--no mountain-climbing, bike riding, activities hard on my feet, yet I am cautious, having just met, and suggest we drive over to Bill's house for the after-dinner business meeting. He agrees.

I wait there, but no Arnie. I check my watch. It's been a half an hour. The night passes, but he does not show up at Bill's.

I'm confused as to what happened. I keep telling myself that perhaps I should have taken the opportunity when it arose and gone on the ride. Perhaps he too has some anxieties about meeting women and I should have acted immediately. By this time, I've been conditioned to accept rejection. Even though a man may not know a thing about me--that I am a published writer, that I have watched the sun disappear in a gondola on the Grand Canal, have raised a son on my own, and outlived many diabetic friends whose fragile stems snapped one by one--I might never get another chance beyond that first encounter. Unfortunately, I end up feeling like I've failed since I've placed the burden of the interaction on myself, on my ability to "snare" him.

One of the side effects of diabetes is psychological--not feeling "as good" as "normal" people. In the business of survival, no one addressed the problem of how diabetics felt about themselves. A deadly second class citizenship persisted throughout my young life. When I was diagnosed at seven young years of age, practitioners only thought of keeping me alive. Yet, compliance was the very thing I dreaded, because it meant being different from others whom I envisioned to be "normal."

Food was my succor and my seducer, ironically opposed to what was intended in a diabetic diet regimen. The idea of staying on a diabetic diet fueled a desire to break it. It became a way of resisting medical practitioners whose rules I didn't fully understand. Ironically, my little rebellions with food formed a bulwark against the fear that I lost control over my life, acts that made me feel in control even when I wasn't.

It takes determination to venture down the road I've set for myself. Is it wise to hope to meet someone in what I consider a broken-down state? Would a man who has lost a wife to illness want a less-than-perfectly healthy second wife? Perhaps it is more comforting to face rejection now than to face it later when I am more involved. After that night, I never hear from Arnie nor see him at social functions again.

The drought of winter extends into periods of inactivity that I try to stem with a fury of exercising three days a week at the Cardiac Rehabilitation Unit of a local hospital. At the Rehab unit's annual dinner dance held at a country club, Jean saves a seat for me, along with several other women. I've worn a black silk pant suit. At the last minute, I decide to wear my Rockports, even though they stick out like a sore thumb.

After dinner, a man taps me on the shoulder, asks if I'd like to dance. He's older, but impeccably dressed in a three-piece navy suit. And he's a fabulous dancer. I amaze myself with jitterbug, the cha cha, even a swing dance. At last a slow one. He introduces himself as "Al." He never looks down at my shoes but I feel uncomfortable about them. "I have trouble with my feet," I say. He smiles, stares straight into my eyes. "I came with Jack Pegeaux," he says, nodding to a familiar face across the room. "His wife was just put in an Alzheimer's unit, and he didn't want to come alone."

At the end of several rounds he asks for my phone number. I write it on a napkin. A week later he calls. It turns out that Al too has had open heart surgery. Yippee! I think; someone who understands. He enjoys cooking, spills out a panoply of delicious dishes he's made. "Maybe I'll have you, Jack, and his new friend over for dinner."

I'm thinking that Jack's poor wife is in an Alzheimer's unit and already he has a "new friend." Gawd! "That's great," I say, the tone in my voice belying my true feelings.

After a long, winding conversation about his children, his wife who passed away, his daughter who died of SIDS, I feel that I can be honest with him. I don't want to get involved with a man and then watch him fall slowly out of love with me when he finds out the truth about my condition. I want facts to be straight from the beginning. I mention that I am a diabetic. Silence follows. Mistake, I'm thinking just as the words leave my mouth, and it is a big one. Al, it turns out, is a male nurse who does private duty work and understands well the impact of the disease on the body. "Oh?" His voice drops an octave. "That's too bad."

Weeks pass and no return call from him. I must admit I am disappointed, rehashing our conversation in my mind. At first, I think, why should he get involved with a woman whose body is booby-trapped, especially when he can meet many women? Every experience like this makes it more difficult to stay positive and not be daunted by the encounter.

Spring comes quickly, and as soon as I see a green sprout in the garden outside my condo, I'm out in the chill March air, digging around. Primroses and daffodils have barely cracked the soil. Snow clings between naked picket hedge like leftover frosting. I'm dressed in my scruffy pants with the padded knees, clearing old leaves trapped in bushes. My nose itches and I try to scratch it with the back of my hand, leaving a smudge behind. I'm sloshing around in my son's old Adidas tennis shoes, hoping that I don't run into anyone. A man walks by, heading for the dumpster, carrying a coffee cup in one hand and a full garbage bag in the other. I run my fingers through tousled hair, pretend to be busy. But the man stops in front of my garden. White haired, his clothes are flawless, just a hint of a white cuff beyond vest sleeves.

"That's quite a plot; do you maintain it or does the super take care of it?"

"No, it's all mine." I keep talking with my head down. "I asked management if I could plant my favorite flowers here."

"So what are your favorites?" he asks.

"Hydrangea, Blue Salvia," I pause figuring he won't know any of them.
"Whatever happened to Delphinium?"

"Oh, I have one. In the back. It's not up yet. Been moved several times.

"My wife had a fondness for Delphinium," he adds then sighs, "looks like a lotta work."

"Yeah, I've got some beautiful things coming up." I say. I don't have any more work in the spot I'm in, and my knees are killing me. I shift around a bit and then give up on hiding the fact that I'm not wearing makeup or a bra. He extends a hand and draws me up, a little too close to escape scrutiny.

"I just moved in two units down from you. My name's Bob Tazza," he says.

I hold up dirt-caked rubber-gloved hands, pull off one, take his hand. It's good to feel a firm grasp. We both pause for a second before disengaging.

"Your hand's freezing," he says. "Why don't you take a break and warm up with some coffee. I just made some."

I try to beg off. "No, I'm really dirty," I say.

"My place is a mess. I've got half opened boxes and paper all over the place, come-on," he insists.

I'm afraid of walking into his place with muddy shoes, and what if I have to take them off, revealing misshapen feet with broken arches. On the other hand, I'm thinking there is something engaging about his grip as he pulled me up and the way he looks me straight in the eye. "Okay," I say.

Boxes block the doorway as we enter the hallway. He clears a path to the livingroom. At the window is a yucca plant. Its leafy head faces the sun, green and brilliant in the yellow light.

THE WHOLE WORLD'S WATCHING – SIBYL JAMES

Whenever I'm in a political demonstration and the crowd begins to chant, "The whole world's watching," I'm transported back to 1968, Chicago, and the Democrats' presidential convention—the first time I heard those admonishing words. I don't know whether the whole world was watching the police attacking the demonstrators outside the convention, but for once the media's cameras were trained on the action, and from where I sat in my parents' living room in central Illinois, I certainly saw those heads get clubbed. I sat in front of the television, fashioning a "hate collage, " magazine and newspaper photos detailing the atrocities of the war on Vietnam. I somehow believed in the power of making such collages, similar to the faith of the protestors who circled the Pentagon, meditating in order to levitate it.

I was barely twenty-two then. Like others at my university, I'd taken to wearing an old green army jacket, donned not in support of the war but as a symbol of dissent. In the cafeteria, I had sat at the table frequented by members of the Students for a Democratic Society (SDS) but I was really only a fellow traveler then. And a critic, attending SDS meetings with a friend and later laughing about the solemn testimonials of the members. I think it was the Democratic Convention that sent me over the edge into real political action. And maybe that's the wonderful thing about Democrats—for all their failings. At least the wonderful thing about Democrats in 1968. It was THEIR convention people thought worth protesting, THEIR venue where dissent might get a hearing. Inside the convention center, the band played "Happy Days Are Here Again." Outside, embattled demonstrators were intent on proving these were not happy days.

I was a privileged radical: white, a college student, and female. I wasn't going to be drafted. I had more in common with Abbey Hoffman and the Yippies' brand of street theatre protest than with the Black Panthers who were paying attention to the idea that all politics is local—and being gunned down by the government for their efforts.

In politics, I was never a leader, but sometimes I fell into it by default—and still do. In 1970, I was quoted by the student newspaper as a spokesperson for the demonstration just because I happened to be there and the reporter happened to pick me to interview. Then, inadvertently, I fell into leadership at an English department meeting when the students at the University of Washington were protesting the U.S. bombing of Cambodia—an auxiliary to the nation's war on Vietnam. It was the first time the department had allowed graduate students to attend a department meeting. I raised my hand to make a motion that we cancel classes in sympathy with student protests. Maybe it's only a figment of my current middle-aged memory, but I recall that the department chair recognized me as "the little lady in the ruffled blouse." Even if that memory is apocryphal, it's accurate—those were the days I wore long skirts, elegant blouses, lots of draping scarves or shawls and the patchouli oil that the department chair confused with the scent of pot.

Somebody seconded my motion, and then it was truth and consequences time: department members had to vote by a show of hands. My motion failed, but afterwards, a real faculty member—as opposed to my negligible graduate student status—thanked me for taking the risk of making that motion. I responded with a quote from Bob Dylan, "If you ain't got nothin,' you got nothin' to lose." Never again did the department invite graduate students to a meeting.

Recently, traveling in Brazil, I woke up with a song from that sixties' Broadway musical *Hair* inexplicably surfacing in my brain—"good morning starshine...nippy nappy loopy, la, la, la, la, la." Today's tattooed and pierced students would consider that sort of song ridiculous. Even I admitted the lyrics were silly. But at breakfast, the *pousada* owner played another song from *Hair*—some kind of international synchronicity, reminding me that this was supposed to be the Age of Aquarius—when peace would rule the planet.

Not all those songs had silly lyrics. I can still picture the ending of the film Milos Forman made of *Hair*, the soldiers walking into the maw of the plane meant to ferry them to Vietnam's hell. I've long thought that hippies were highly moral people—despite the sex, drugs and rock and roll propaganda. We had a vision that refused war and hypocrisy, drove VW vans instead of SUVs. At 63, I'm an old hippie, wearing a t-shirt with the latest version of SDS: Seniors for a Democratic Society. Despite my bouts of cynicism, I still believe that if we fight hard enough, march long enough, peace will rule the planet, and love will steer the stars—just like that song from *Hair* promised.

THE BATH – HOLLY J. HUGHES

The tub fills inch by inch,
as I kneel beside it, trail my fingers
in the bright braid of water.
Mom perches on the toilet seat,
entranced by the ritual until
she realizes the bath's for her.
Oh no, she says, drawing her
three layers of shirts to her chest,
crossing her arms and legs.
Oh no, I couldn't, she repeats,
brow furrowing, that look I now
recognize like an approaching squall.
I abandon reason, the hygiene argument,
promise a Hershey's bar, if she will just,
please, take off her clothes. *Oh no*,
she repeats, her voice rising.
Meanwhile, the water is cooling.
I strip off my clothes, step into it,
let the warm water take me
completely, slipping down until
only my face shines up, a moon mask.
Mom stays with me, interested now
in this turn of events. I sit up.
Will you wash my back, Mom?
So much gone, but let this
still be there. She bends over
to dip the washcloth in the still
warm water, squeezes it,
lets it dribble down my back,
leans over to rub the butter pat
of soap, swiping each armpit,
then rinses off the suds with long
practiced strokes. I turn around
to thank her, catch her smiling,
lips pursed, humming,
still a mother with a daughter
whose back needs washing.

RECOVERY – JULIE L. MOORE

Walking along my front porch, I rub my swollen
    belly like I did, years ago, when I was expecting

a miracle. I am empty now, gutted
    like the old farmhouse across the street,

every room pared down to the frame's
    bare bones. Even the floors have been removed.

All I anticipate now is a day when pain
    breaks. I've had seven surgeries—

adhesions excised like splinters,
    four rundown organs

pulled out like windows and walls.
    Here in mid-life, I'm nothing but pure

ruin. And part of me would like to give up,
    dissolve into dust like my neighbor's brick.

But in the ash trees that line our road,
    in flawless iambs, the sparrows chant

preserve, preserve, preserve, preserve.
    And I step into our yard where bees,

persistent as repeated pleas,
    poise themselves before the roses,

then bury their faces in the velvet
    breasts, suckling sugar, tasting

grace as insistent as the tune they hum.

HOPKINTOWN IOWA – KAY MULLEN

My sister and I return after many years to our grandmother's house where we lived after mother died. The house stands apologetic, the stone porch and chimney covered with stains, French windows smudged under dark-webbed eaves.

Behind the house, in the same barn where the Fiddler boys snapped the necks of sparrows, the elderly woman who now occupies the house, sits in a canvas chair sorting junk. Stockings sag around her ankles. She greets us, then rambles on about the barn's contents, the three-legged stool she squatted on for milking, a plow and harness once attached to a single wagon tree, forks for pitching hay, a rusty hoe. Pausing, she offers to lead us to the house. "Avoid the kitchen," she says. Compared to litter of the house, the barn becomes a pale reflection, every room crowded with boxes, buckets of empty bottles and Mason jars, spools of ribbon and string. Stacks of old newspapers line a path to the living room where the woman slumps in a broken rocker beside the fireplace.

....sitting beside the hearth in his favorite chair, my grandfather pokers the dying coals into flames. His smoking-stand holds matches he snaps as he cups one hand around his favorite pipe, the sweet aroma, perfect rings circling our upturned heads. I taste after dinner treats under over-turned plates, pull strings of the butterfly lamp for a bedtime story, snuggle with my grandmother on the piano bench as she plays and sings. At naptime I climb back stairs to a rag doll and darkened rooms, trace circles with spit on the bedroom mirror. I shout at the pigeons fluttering on hidden ledges of chimney stones, in morning, smell fresh Kolachkes and coffee wafting upstairs.

My sister taps me on the shoulder. We step to the porch into Iowa's sultry air. I hear my grandmother's voice in the *coo* of a mourning dove.

WILD LOVE – MARJORIE ROMMEL

Mate caught in a trap, she looks
for ways to release him, fetches

small game for his sustenance,
soaks up river water to bring him drink

in her fur. She curls around him
at night, licks his wound, soothing

his coat & his heart; they sing together
in darkness. She stays, she stays

till death shows him mercy, or he
gnaws the caught leg free.

COMFORT FOOD – LISA OHLEN HARRIS

I woo Jeanne's appetite with her favorite foods. Grits, banana pudding, Miracle Whip and bologna loaf on white bread. French dressing over cottage cheese. Sausage gravy over biscuits: pallid sauce so thick with grease that the leftovers will congeal, gray and lumpy. Tomorrow I will reheat them to mash over her toast.

When she first moved in with us I made things my way: stir fry, one-pot dishes, beans and rice. She ate only after fishing out the veggies. If I used tofu, she asked, "What's this stuff?" and pushed it aside. And yet she bragged, "Lisa is such a good cook!" Years passed and I learned to reserve a handful of raw veggies for her plate; she loved vegetables, as it ended up—just not cooked.

Back when I was Todd's girlfriend, Jeanne invited her minister and his wife, among others, to a dinner party. She cut the greens quickly with scissors and tossed the salad in a large trash bag. She made the entire meal a day ahead, so when the guests arrived we all were relaxed and ready, and all she had to do was reheat. I remember chicken Parmesan that night, a salad with honeyed almonds and red onions. I remember the smell of garlic cheese bread rising as the minister said grace. I remember bringing the savory bread to my mouth and crunching in to find that instead of garlic butter under the melted cheese she had spread Miracle Whip, warm and cloying. After a long wash of ice water to get the hunk down, I poked at the rest of my meal.

Once I had a ring on my finger, I volunteered to make the cheese bread whenever she cooked Italian. And when I had the Harris name firmly attached by vows to my own, I also picked the red onions out of my salad and laid them on the side of my plate.

In recipes calling for milk I now substitute heavy cream. My mother-in-law has lost seven pounds in two weeks and we're not sure why, except the doctor says the mass in her lungs—three months ago the size of the doctor's retractable pen clicker—is now the size of both his hands fisted one over the other.

What the tests will show, what the future will be, I do not know—what I do know is this: break the sausage apart as it fries in the pan; sprinkle in flour to absorb the grease; add heavy cream and stir until the sauce is thick and no lumps remain. Spoon the mixture over biscuits or toast and grind fresh pepper on top. When I bring it to her, the plate will be warm through. She will take and eat.

URN – MARCI AMELUXEN

                They said *urn*
at the mortuary but it was a can
shocking when laid in my hands
                  her years of life
dust to sift in a metal tube.

        Like a kaleidoscope
I hold the can to my eye, see
spring flowers, a paint brush   (turn)
              bread, bottle of whiskey, music
(turn)   scraped elbows, kisses.

              How can we imagine the body
enkindled, cracked to immeasurable pieces
soul left to remake
                  itself to colors

            bones of the hand white
July 4th sparklers
red engine behind the hand
        pulsing, then still

where to locate her last song
cup between palms its breath
                and note

where to press and leave my print
on her tan flesh.

ON NOT PIVOTING – LIA PURPURA

Not that I haven't *known* "pivotal." Not that I haven't myself pivoted: indeed, I've turned from one state of being to another so fast, so hard, that g-forces waggled my cheeks and pinned me to walls, chairs, floors, countries. And it's not that I fear my Pivotal Life Events might pale in comparison to others' PLEs. It's just that I work best in quanta and jots. PLEs are constructed pointillistically for me and I am best returned to the country of myself by way of micromoments.

Maybe my PLE's aren't the talkative kind, or are, but I'm not especially calibrated to receive the momentous. Sometimes I feel that moments others might construe as "pivotal" on my behalf, should exert more force than they do, should fit more neatly into a Big Life Narrative. (In fact, in college, I tried on some popular BLNs using the PC lingo of the day—but I couldn't crank the drama up high enough, and I kept feeling I should have been more wrecked than I was by certain PLEs – to effect the proper pivot into Meaning.) My PLEs don't emit much reverb. They aren't shiny, flashy, reflective; timely or hip or twitter-worthy, though likely in another's hands they would be spiffed up and sent forth with proper fanfare and frame. It's mysterious to me, the power of smallish-seeming things up against the eruptive volcanics. Honestly, it's not there haven't been Big Moments – it's just that after a while, things come back the same size. Caught in the same tide, everything rolls in and out together. Everything tends towards the pebbly.

I could do Pivotal Friendships. Pivotal Animals I Have Known. Pivotal Whole Years, Surgeries, Mean Girls. Escapes and Near-Misses, foreign and domestic. Epic Dumbness. Luck-Beyond-Reason. But a "pivot" (which, now that I've said it so many times, sounds like "divot" -- a little dug-out gouge where shadows are kept, in a chin or cheek, or on a playing field) implies a sharp turning from one place, stage, way of being, to another. And I've rarely snapped to attention like that, even in hindsight (though I always liked militaristic turning-on-heels as a kid, that faux snapping-to-attention, so not my family's way, and by which my son, now taller than me, mocks my orders to hurry up.)

I don't mean to be contrary. I understand the assignment here. I mean only to respond authentically to the suggestion that Pivotal Moments are the proper/substantial building blocks of a life or an art. Why am I so resistant? Do I lack a gene for spectacle? (It's true, to be fair, I'm not drawn to memoir myself, though I can recommend many fine ones– among them Sven Birkert's *My Sky Blue Trades* and William Davies King *Collections of Nothing* – works in which both writers conduct into the self-on-the-page the zeitgeists and milieus that shape us all.) Have I simply been luckier, less impinged-upon or hurt than others – and thus no PLEs rumble and crest? Am I more forgetful? More forgiving? So susceptible to overwhelm that I'm inclined to flatten the peaks and troughs, producing a vastly smoother landscape for the compiling mind to traverse?

Maybe it's more my resistance to ranking, too aware of the fact that choosing one PLE for first place in the line up precludes, reduces, scuttles other good choices and possible orders. I'm wary about setting the stones of "my story." Reluctant to build the path in hindsight. Of course I have my important oceans, lost friendships, travel mishaps, stunning books, fateful decisions, crashes, regrets, family moments. But in the most daily way, I don't think of the Bigs as making up what I know of as my "self." (How nice it might be, though, to have 3 good PLEs on which to hang my hat, coat, reputation. To point and refer to, revise myself by. To lead, name and order me. Form, plump, pare and turn me. Be my net. Be my ladder.)

And there's the heart of it: the way in which a self constitutes itself *daily* supersedes the PLEs. So, daily, caught in the act of sketching in the self I know myself to be, I'd be more likely to think of: the yellow speckly breakfast table rimmed with a shiny lip of aluminum in my grandmother's and great aunt's breakfast room (a little nook with benches just off the kitchen) which returns me to that long period of running my finger along the silver edge (childhood), and the surprise bursting open of scenes that comes by way of recalling the feel of the metal, the gold flecks floating in a buttery expanse (quick veer into extended yellow: those stretchy Danskin pants/shirt sets we all wore; my shock -- edge of my bed, late afternoon, open closet-- when once my mother suggested we buy a black sweater; black was for grown-ups! *How could my otherwise sensitive mother not know that?* And just one more veering, via mention-of-black: my black pumps, the French ones, my first, with the ice-blue leather lining, very low cut in front, with a kitten heel. How perfectly elegant they made me feel, or rather, how by way of them, I located "elegance" for the first time, the sensation very like a sharp hunger.)

Back in the breakfast room, there are violets on the windowsill, Sweet 'n Low packets in a Lucite holder (oh Lucite craze of the 70s, the school fairs at which we bought such tchotchkes for our parents), toaster, radio, deck of cards, cut coupons, nail file, scissors, pen, all arranged on a plastic tray. Wooden napkin box hung on the wall. Green flowered wall paper, unwilted by years. By way of these things, here comes the sense of my self as a girl, the ways I felt myself in the world – kept whole by objects recollected, and returned to me anytime, at a red light, while walking the dog, vast and surprising.

Surely all the meals I ate there *"made me who I am today."* As much as any Single Defining Event, the years of breakfasts with my grandmother and aunt, cakes, muffins, bacon (we never had bacon in our house), bickering (it was called and thus blessed with minorness), the cream in a glass jar, butter on everything, gum under the table stuck there by my mother as a child. My uncle's scrawly name written in pen underneath. That the stuck gum was naughtier than the scrawled name, consider the accretion of stories, sighs, comments and stances that would have led me to that determination . . .

And I could go on. I could walk for miles right now, fielding all that passes through, rubs off, lends a sense of being – that rush of moments, objects, sensations so much like a cloud of gnats, mist, rain, hail, cold patch in the ocean, dust motes in a ray of sun that roil, gather, settle around my head a and make up the daily weather of a self.

CONTRIBUTORS

Dilruba Ahmed is the author of Dhaka Dust (Graywolf, 2011), winner of the 2010 Bakeless Literary Prize for poetry awarded by the Bread Loaf Writers' Conference. Her poetry has appeared in Blackbird , Cream City Review, New England Review, New Orleans Review, and Pebble Lake Review, and Indivisible: Contemporary South Asian American Poetry. A writer with roots in Pennsylvania, Ohio, and Bangladesh, Ahmed holds BPhil and MAT degrees from the University of Pittsburgh and an MFA from Warren Wilson College.

Huda Al-Marashi is an Iraqi-American at work on a memoir from which "Deal with it Madame" is an excerpt. Other excerpts from this memoir appear in the anthologies *In Her Place* and *Love Inshallah: The Secret Love Lives of Muslim American Women*. Her poem, *TV Terror*, is a part of a touring exhibit commemorating the Mutanabbi Street Bombing in Baghdad. She is the recipient of a 2012 Creative Workforce Fellowship, a program of the Community Partnership for Arts and Culture, made possible by the generous support of Cuyahoga County citizens through Cuyahoga Art and Culture.

Marci Ameluxen's poems have appeared or are forthcoming in *The Comstock Review, Waccamaw, Passager, The Compass Rose, The Dirty Napkin, The Mom Egg, Off Channel* and *Hospital Drive*. Her chapbook manuscript "The Daughter Speaks" received Honorable Mention in the Clockwise Chapbook Competition 2010; and was semifinalist in the Goldline Press Chapbook Competition, 2010.

Ellen Bass has published several previous volumes of poetry, including *The Human Line*, (Copper Canyon, 2007, and *Mules of Love* (BOA, 2002) which won the Lambda Literary Award. She was awarded the Elliston Book Award for Poetry from the University of Cincinnati, *Nimrod*/Hardman's Pablo Neruda Prize, *The Missouri Review's* Larry Levis Award, the Greensboro Poetry Prize, the New Letters Poetry Prize, the Chautauqua Poetry Prize, a Pushcart Prize, and a Fellowship from the California Arts Council.

Marilyn Bates author of *It Could Drive You Crazy*, is a "Poet in Person" with the International Poetry Forum, and a fellow of the National Writing Project at the University of Pittsburgh. Her work has appeared in *The MacGuffin*, *The Paterson Literary Review*, *One Trick Pony*, *Poet Lore*, and *The Potomac Review*. Her play, *Life Without Nipples*, was produced by the Pittsburgh New Works Theater Festival.

Jennifer Brennock earned her MFA in Creative Writing from Goddard College. She writes and teaches in the San Juan Islands. An excerpt from her memoir, *Barren*, was recently published in the *Pitkin Review* and *Line Zero*. Her novel in progress, *Not Jewish*, is the story of a family refusing to blend. Jennifer's Trigger Happy at jenniferbrennock.blogspot.com.

Michelle Cacho-Negrete's essays appear in *The Sun*'s new book *The Mysterious Life of the Heart* and in *Thoreau's Legacy*. Her essay "Heat" was selected as one of the 100 most notable essays of 2004. She has been published in a number of magazines, including *The Sun Magazine*, *Wisconsin Review*, and *Gulf Stream*. She won the Hope Award, and has been nominated four times for a Pushcart Prize.

Jennifer Chapis has published in magazines and anthologies such as *American Letters & Commentary*, *Best New Poets*, *Colorado Review*, *The Iowa Review*, *McSweeney's*, *North American Review*, and *Verse*. She was awarded the Arts & Letters Rumi Prize in Poetry chosen by Mark Doty and the Backwards City Poetry Series Prize for her chapbook, *The Beekeeper's Departure*. Faculty at New York University and Co-founder of Nightboat Books, Jennifer lives in Brooklyn.

Kerri French's poetry has been featured on Sirius Satellite Radio and was selected for inclusion in Best New Poets 2008. A recipient of the Larry Franklin and Mei Kwong Fellowship from the Writers' Room of Boston, her poetry has appeared in Barrow Street, The Southeast Review, Fugue, and Lumina, among others. She holds an MFA in Creative Writing from UNC-Greensboro and has taught writing and literature at Boston University, Mount Ida College, and UNC-Greensboro.

Christin Geall teaches nonfiction at the University of Victoria, in British Columbia. Her work has been selected by *Creative*

Nonfiction and recently appeared in *Walk Myself Home, 21st Century Motherhood*, and *Women Writing on Family: Tips on Writing, Teaching and Publishing*. 'The Jumper' is excerpted from Christin's work-in-progress, Fill Her Up: A Memoir of Money, Motherhood and Desire. www.christingeall.com

Adrian Gibbons Koesters holds an MFA degree from the Rainier Writing Workshop at Pacific Lutheran University and a Ph.D. in creative writing from the University of Nebraska-Lincoln. She is the author of the nonfiction work *Healing Mysteries*, published in 2005 by Paulist Press. Her poems have appeared in *The International Poetry Review, Crab Creek Review, A River and Sound Review*, and elsewhere.

Jennifer Gibson is a social worker whose poem "Apostrophe S" was a finalist in the 2010 Joy Bale Boone Poetry Prize and published in "The Heartland Review." Her work has also appeared in "Pegasus," "Limestone," "JAR," and "Open 24 Hours," among others. In 2008, she was a finalist in The Next Great Writers Competition. She has received two summer writers residencies from the Kentucky Foundation of Women.

D.L. Hall is the author of *The Anatomy of Narrative: Analyzing Fiction and Creative Nonfiction* and has published her writing in *The Literary Review: An International Journal of Contemporary Writing, The Sun, River Teeth: A Journal of Nonfiction Narrative, Arkansas Review*, and *Apalachee Review* among others. She received her PhD in English from Florida State University in 2004 and currently teaches at Valdosta State University in Georgia.

Kelly Hayes-Raitt was press credentialed by the Jordanian government as she entered Iraq in July 2003, three months after the US-led invasion. She reported live from Baghdad, Fallouja and Basra via satellite phone to National Public Radio, KNBC-TV and other news outlets. Her essays about Iraqi refugees appear in several anthologies including Random House's *Female Nomad & Friends* and *Best Women's Travel Writing 2011*. "Getting Bombed" is from her forthcoming journalistic memoir *Living Large in Limbo: How I Found Myself Among the World's Forgotten*. An award-winning author, she lectures at colleges and other venues, lives in Los Angeles and Ajijic, Mexico, and blogs at www.PeacePATHFoundation.org.

Julie Hensley grew up in the Shenandoah Valley of Virginia. She lived in Arizona for several years before settling in Kentucky where she currently makes her home with her husband (the writer R. Dean Johnson) and their son. Her poems and stories have appeared in many journals, including *Indiana Review, Redivider, Phoebe, Ellipsis,* and *Ruminate*. She is a member of the core faculty of the brief residency MFA program at Eastern Kentucky University.

Beatrice M. Hogg is a freelance writer living in Sacramento, California. She has a MFA degree in Creative Nonfiction from Antioch University Los Angeles. Her stories about her father have appeared in *Coal People, Reminisce, The Sacramento Bee* and the anthology *Our Black Fathers: Brave, Bold and Beautiful*. She is working on several essay collections and a novel.

Holly J. Hughes is the editor of the award-winning anthology, *Beyond Forgetting: Poetry and Prose about Alzheimer's Disease*, published by Kent State University Press and the author of *Boxing the Compass*, published by Floating Bridge Press. Nominated for several Pushcart prizes, her poems and essays have appeared in many anthologies. *The Pen and the Bell: Mindful Writing in a Busy World*, a collaboration with essayist Brenda Miller, is forthcoming from Skinner House Press. A graduate of Pacific Lutheran University's MFA program, she has taught writing workshops at Fishtrap, North Cascades Institute, Edmonds Write on the Sound, Rainier Writers Workshop and Field's End, among others.

Sibyl James's publications include nine books (fiction, poetry, and travel memoirs), plus individual works in over 100 journals internationally. Her writing has received awards from Artist Trust and the Seattle, King County, and Washington State arts commissions. She has a PhD in English and has taught in the U.S., Mexico, China, and-- as Fulbright professor--Tunisia and Cote d'Ivoire.

Jill N. Kandel has lived in Zambia, Indonesia, England, and in her husband's native Netherlands. She currently lives in Minnesota, with her husband and children, where she edits and writes for *Area Woman* magazine and teaches journaling to inmates at the local county jail. Her writing has been published in literary journals including *The*

Gettysburg Review, Brevity, River Teeth, Image, and *The Pinch.* One of her essays was published in the anthology *The Best Spiritual Writing 2012.*

Chavawn Kelley lives at 7,200 feet in Laramie, Wyoming. Her prose and poetry have appeared in numerous anthologies, including *Thoreau's Legacy: American Stories about Global Warming,* and in journals such as *Creative Nonfiction, High Desert Journal, The Iowa Review* and *Terrain.org.* She has received support from the Wyoming Arts Council, the Ucross Foundation, the Ludwig Vogelstein Foundation, and Can Serrat International Arts Center (Spain).

Lita Kurth's identity as a spiritual progressive sprang from opposing directions: a church-hopping father who gave her a religious education extending from Christian Science to Foursquare Gospel, and an impoverished childhood with heated discussions of world affairs. A deep look at her own psycho-spiritual difficulties nudged her toward a political engagement informed by love and truth (a Jungian integration of opposites). Educated at UW Madison, UC Berkeley, San Francisco State, and Pacific Lutheran University, Lita teaches Composition and leads creative writing workshops.

Rebecca Lauren teaches English at Eastern University. Her poetry has been published or is forthcoming in *Prairie Schooner, Mid-American Review, The Journal of Feminist Studies in Religion, Southeast Review, Calyx* and *The Cincinnati Review,* among others. Her chapbook, *The Schwenkfelders,* was co-winner of the 2009 Keystone Chapbook Prize and is available through Seven Kitchens Press <sevenkitchenspress.wordpress.com>.

Anna Leahy is the author of *Constituents of Matter,* winner of the Wick Poetry Prize in 2006. Her poetry has appeared in journals such as the *Connecticut Review, Crab Orchard Review, The Journal* and *Phoebe.* Leahy is editor of *Power and Identity in the Creative Writing Classroom,* which launched the New Writing Viewpoints series. *Lofty Ambitions,* the blog she co-authors with Doug Dechow explores aviation, science in the twentieth century and writing as a couple. Leahy is the director of Tabula Poetica and an Associate Professor of English at Chapman University in Orange, California.

Susan Leahy is a wife and mother of three. Originally from The Bronx, New York, she has grown roots in Wickford, Rhode Island. She and her family live a creative home schooling lifestyle. She loves hard alternative rock, making jewelry, collecting skulls and antlers, is a passionate genealogist and looks forward to writing the story of the family. This is her first writing submission and first acceptance.

Dinah Lenney wrote *Bigger than Life: A Murder, a Memoir* (American Lives, University of Nebraska Press), and co-authored *Acting for Young Actors*. Her essays have appeared in *Creative Nonfiction, the Kenyon Review Online, Agni, The Los Angeles Review of Books, Ploughshares, Water~Stone, the New York Times* and elsewhere. Dinah teaches in the Rainer Writing Workshop, the Bennington Writing Seminars, and the Master of Professional Writing program at USC.

Emily Levine is a freshman and chancellor scholar at the Dodge College of Film at Chapman University, majoring in Public Relations and Advertising. She is a first-time author from California.

Ellaraine Lockie writes poetry, nonfiction books and essays. She has received writing residencies at Centrum, twelve Pushcart Prize nominations, and several hundred awards for her poetry. Her chapbook, *Stroking David's Leg*, received the Best Individual Collection Award for 2010 from *Purple Patch* magazine in England, and her chapbook, *Red for the Funeral*, won the 2010 San Gabriel Poetry Festival Chapbook Contest. Her ninth chapbook, *Wild as in Familiar*, was a finalist in the recent Finishing Line Press chapbook contest, and has been released there. She teaches poetry/writing workshops and serves as Poetry Editor for the lifestyles magazine, *Lilipoh*.

Margie Lukas grew up on a farm in central Nebraska. She received her BFA at the University of Nebraska-Omaha and her MFA from the Rainier Writer's Workshop in Tacoma Washington. Her award winning short story, "The Yellow Bird," was produced and premiered at the Cannes Film Festival in France in 2005. She is an instructor in the Writer's Workshop at the University of Nebraska-Omaha and a sometimes-contributor to *NEBRASKAland* Magazine. She is a recipient of a Nebraska Arts Council Fellowship Award.

Kathleen Lynch is the author of *Hinge* (Black Zinnias National Poetry Prize), and chapbooks *How to Build an Owl* (Select Poet Series prize, Small Poetry Press), *No Spring Chicken* (White Eagle Coffee Store Press Prize), *Alterations of Rising* (Small Poetry Press Select Poet Series), *Kathleen Lynch-Greatest Hits* (Pudding House Publications-invitational series). Her work is included in several major anthologies and college textbooks. Web site: www.kathleenlynch.com

Marjorie Manwaring is a freelance writer and an editor for the online poetry and art journal the *DMQ Review*. Her chapbook *What to Make of a Diminished Thing* is forthcoming from Dancing Girl Press in 2012, and her first full-length collection, *Search for a Velvet-lined Cape*, is forthcoming from Mayapple Press in 2013. She has been awarded writing residencies through the Whiteley Center at Friday Harbor on San Juan Island and Artsmith on Orcas Island. Marjorie won the Artsmith Literary Award in 2010.

Carolyn A. Martin is a happily retired educator and author whose poems have appeared in publications such as *Christian Century, Drash: Northwest Mosaic, The Naugatuck River Review,* and *VoiceCatcher*. Her first collection, *Finding Compass*, was released by Queen of Wands Press (Portland, Oregon) in July 2011. Currently, she writes, dreams, and gardens in Clackamas, Oregon.

Nancy McKinley's writing appears in *The Cortland Review*, Issue 53, *Main Street Rag Short Fiction Anthologies: Commutability*, Pushcart nomination, *Coming Home, Big Water,* and in *Colorado Review*. She has taught English and Women's Studies and is a founding faculty member of the M.A/.M.F.A. at Wilkes University. Presentations include AWP 2011, *Online Mentoring for Writers and Interns* and AWP 2007, *Unsung Litany of Late Blooming Writers*. She earned her Ph.D. from SUNY-Binghamton, M.A. from Colorado State University, and B.A. from College of the Holy Cross where she was one of the first females at the previously male school.

Julie L. Moore is the author of *Slipping Out of Bloom* (WordTech Editions, 2010), and *Election Day* (Finishing Line Press, 2006). Moore is the Writing Center Director at Cedarville University in Cedarville, Ohio, where she lives with her husband John; children, Ashley and

Alex; and their beloved Black Lab Maggie. More information about Moore's work is available at julielmoore.com.

Kay Mullen's work has appeared in *Appalachia, American Life in Poetry, Crab Creek Review, Valparaiso Poetry Review, Blue Unicorn, Shark Reef Poetry Journal* and others as well as Anthologies: *In Tahoma's Shadow, Beyond Forgetting* and *Floating Bridge Review*. She has authored two full length poetry books, *Let Morning Begin* (2001) and *A Long Remembering: Return to Vietnam* (2006). Several of her poems have been nominated for the Pushcart Prize, as well as Sundress Publications' Best of the Net 2009. Kay earned the Rainier Writing Workshop MFA from Pacific Lutheran University.

Nancy J. Nordenson holds an MFA in creative writing from Seattle Pacific University. Her essay "Ontology" received "notable" recognition in *The Best American Essays 2010*. Other work has been published in *Indiana Review, Under the Sun, Lake Effect, Comment, Relief, Saint Katherine Review,* and the anthology, *The Spirit of Food* (Cascade Press, 2010). She is also the author of *Just Think: Nourish Your Mind to Feed Your Soul* (Baker, 2004). She lives in Minneapolis with her husband.

Lisa Ohlen Harris is the author of the Middle East memoir *Through the Veil*. She lives in a small college town in northwestern Oregon, where she teaches English as a Second Language.

Elaine Neil Orr, an award-winning professor of literature and creative writing at North Carolina State University, was born and spent most of her childhood in Nigeria where her parents were medical missionaries. She is the author of *Gods of Noonday: A White Girl's African Life* (Virginia, a *Book Sense* selection); her recent short fiction and memoir appear in *The Missouri Review, Shenandoah, Blackbird*, and *Image*, among other places. She has been three times nominated for a Pushcart Prize and has won fellowships from the North Carolina Arts Council and the NEH. In addition to her creative writing, Orr is the author of *Tillie Olsen and a Feminist Spiritual Vision* and *Subject to Negotiation: Reading Feminist Criticism and American Women's Writing*.

Anne Pekuri has made her home on an island in the Pacific Northwest where she raised three daughters, works, writes, gardens and begins journeys to faraway places.

Nadine France Martine Pinede is the daughter of Haitian immigrants. She was educated at Harvard, Oxford, and Indiana University, where she received her PhD in Philosophy of Education. She is the author of *A Geography of Hope* (Finishing Line Press), and her short fiction was published in *Haiti Noir*, edited by Edwidge Danticat. Her work has been nominated for a Pushcart Prize and shortlisted for the Hurston-Wright College Writers Award. Nadine is the recipient of fellowships from the Elizabeth George Foundation, the Atlantic Center for the Arts, Hedgebrook Retreat for Women Writers, and the Indiana Arts Commission.

Andrea Potos is the author of *Abundance to Share With the Birds* from Finishing Line Press, *Yaya's Cloth* from Iris Press, *The Perfect Day* from Parallel Press, and a full-length poetry collection, *We Lit the Lamps Ourselves*, from Salmon Poetry of Ireland.

Lia Purpura's recent books include *On Looking* (essays, Sarabande Books), a Finalist for the National Book Critics Circle Award, and *King Baby* (poems, Alice James Books), winner of the Beatrice Hawley Award. Her awards include NEA and Fulbright Fellowships, three Pushcart prizes, work in *Best American Essays, 2011*, the AWP Award in Nonfiction, and the Ohio State University Press Award in Poetry. Recent work appears in *Agni, Field, The Georgia Review, Orion, The New Republic, The New Yorker, The Paris Review,* and elsewhere. She is Writer in Residence at Loyola University, Baltimore, MD and teaches in the Rainier Writing Workshop MFA Program. Her latest collection of essays is *Rough Likeness* (Sarabande Books, 2012)

Marjorie Rommel has taught poetry at Pacific Lutheran University (PLU), Tacoma, Washington, and creative writing at Highline Community College, Des Moines, Washington, and Pierce Community College, Puyallup, Washington. She was a Willard R. Espy Literary Foundation poetry resident in 2000, and received an Adam Family Foundation White Bridge Traveling Fellowship to live and write in Teton Valley, Idaho, in 2001. She is a great-grandmother and sole caregiver for her husband, has two cats, a large garden, a great many more books than easily fit into her small house, a few poems in good places, and an MFA from the Rainier Writing Workshop at PLU.

Marjorie Saiser was named Distinguished Artist in Poetry in 2009 by the Nebraska Arts Council. She received her MA in creative writing at the University of Nebraska—Lincoln. Her first book, *Bones of a Very Fine Hand* (Backwaters Press, 1999), won the Nebraska Book Award. She co-edited *Times of Sorrow. Times of Grace*, an anthology of writing by women of the Great Plains, as well as a book of interviews, *Road Trip: Conversations with Writers* (both from Backwaters Press). Her most recent collection is *Beside You at the Stoplight* (The Backwaters Press, 2010), winner of the Little Bluestem Award.

Peggy Shumaker is the Alaska State Writer Laureate. Her most recent book of poems is *Gnawed Bones*. Her lyrical memoir is *Just Breathe Normally*. Professor emerita at University of Alaska Fairbanks, she teaches in the Rainier Writing Workshop and at many writing conferences and festivals. She earned her B.A. in English and M.F.A. in Creative Writing from the University of Arizona. Peggy founded Boreal Books, an imprint of Red Hen Press, to publish literature and fine art from Alaska. She was awarded a National Endowment for the Arts Fellowship in Poetry. She's active on the National Advisory Board for the *Prairie Schooner* Book Prizes and the Advisory Board of Red Hen Press. Peggy is a contributing editor of *Alaska Quarterly Review*. She has served as poet in residence at the Stadler Center for Poetry at Bucknell and as the president of the board of directors of AWP.

SJ Sindu was born in Sri Lanka and came to the U.S. at the age of seven. Ze writes fiction, nonfiction, poetry, and cultural criticism focused on the experiences of minority voices. Hir work strives to represent those who live on the margins of society and in the borderlands between identities.

Judith Slater has a BA from the University of Oregon, MA from San Francisco State, and the MFA from the University of Massachusetts — Amherst. She is the 1998 winner of the Mary McCarthy Prize in Short Fiction from Sarabande Books, publishers of her collection *The Baby Can Sing* (1999). Her stories have appeared in Beloit Fiction

Journal, Redbook, Colorado Review, Greensboro Review, and other places. She teaches creative writing and literature and serves as a reader for *Prairie Schooner* at the University of Nebraska — Lincoln. She has received two awards from the Nebraska Arts Council.

Sheila Squillante is the author of the poetry chapbook, *A Woman Traces the Shoreline* (Dancing Girl Press, 2011). Her work has appeared in places like *Phoebe, Cream City Review, No Tell Motel, Quarterly West, Prairie Schooner, Connecticut Review, The Southeast Review, Glamour, Brevity, Literary Mama*, and elsewhere. She has been a fellow at the MacDowell Colony and the Virginia Center for the Creative Arts, and, in 2009, received a Pushcart nomination for her work. She lives with her family in Central Pennsylvania and teaches writing at Penn State.

Keli Stewart's writing has appeared in *Quiddity, Meridians, Naugatuck River Review, Warpland: A Journal of Black Literature and Ideas, Calyx, Reverie* and *Spaces Between Us*, among other notable journals. She has received artist fellowships from Hedgebrook, where she was awarded the 2010 Adrienne Reiner Hochstadt Award, and the Augusta Savage Gallery's Arts International Residency Program. She was awarded the first place 2010 Gwendolyn Brooks Poetry Award from the Illinois Center for the Book Emerging Writers Prize and is also an alum of the Voices of Our Nation Arts Foundation and Callaloo Summer Writing Workshops. She is currently at work on her first poetry collection.

Jenelle Tabor earned a Master of Public Administration in 2009 from Seattle University. She has worked as an advocate for people with mental illness, low income families, and education for the underserved.

Maria Terrone is the author of two poetry collections: *A Secret Room in Fall*, co-winner of the McGovern Prize (Ashland Poetry Press, 2006) and *The Bodies We Were Loaned* (The Word Works), and a chapbook, *American Gothic, Take 2*. Her work, winner of awards from *Passages North, Willow Review* and *Wind*, has been published in French and Farsi and appeared in such magazines as *The Hudson Review, Poetry, Notre Dame Review,* and *Poetry International*. Over a dozen anthologies have featured her poetry, including the best-selling *Killer Verse: Poems of Murder and Mayhem* (Knopf Everyman series). Visit her at www.mariaterrone.com.

Tammy Tillotson lives in Chase City, VA with her husband and two small tireless boys. Her poetry has recently appeared in *Chopin with Cherries: A Tribute in Verse* and *Sweetbay Review*. Her poem "The Book of POD" won Honorable Mention in the 2009 Wergle Flomp Humor Poetry Contest. She earned her Master of Arts in Liberal Studies from Hollins University.

Bibi Wein divides her time between Manhattan and a log cabin in the Adirondack mountains. She is the author of three books and numerous essays, profiles and short stories. Her work has appeared in *Iris, American Letters & Commentary, Hawk and Handsaw, Other Voices, Kalliope, Biography,* and many other magazines and anthologies. Twice a Pushcart Prize nominee, Bibi has been a fellow of The New York Foundation for the Arts, Virginia Center for the Creative Arts, Blue Mountain Center, Artsmith, and Yaddo. She is currently working on a sequel to her memoir, *The Way Home: A Wilderness Odyssey,* which received the Tupelo Press Editor's Award for Prose.

Sherrie Weller teaches writing at Loyola University, and has an MFA in Creative Writing from the University of Minnesota.

Susan White, originally from eastern Tennessee, received her Masters degree from the Bread Loaf School of English and her MFA from Stonecoast. She teaches high school English in Asheville, North Carolina. When she's not grading or writing, Susan enjoys running on the mountain trails with her dogs, Zora, Callie, and Hooper. She has published fiction and nonfiction in *Fresh Boiled Peanuts, Front Range Review, River Walk Journal, Diverse Voices, Barely South Review, Pisgah Review,* and the anthology *Dear John, I Love Jane*.

JILL MCCABE JOHNSON

Jill McCabe Johnson is the director of Artsmith, a non-profit to support the arts. She is the recipient of the Paula Jones Gardiner Award in Poetry, the *ScissorTale Review* Editor's Prize in Poetry, a fellowship from the Deborah Tall Memorial Fund, a residency from the A.P. Anderson Center, and Pushcart nominations in poetry, fiction, and nonfiction. Her writing has appeared in journals such as *The Los Angeles Review*, *Iron Horse Literary Review*, *Brevity*, *Prairie Schooner*, and *Harpur Palate*. She earned her MFA from the Rainier Writing Workshop at Pacific Lutheran University, and is pursuing a PhD in English at the University of Nebraska. She lives with her husband on an island in the Salish Sea.

CPSIA information can be obtained
at www.ICGtesting.com
Printed in the USA
LVHW041726050320
649105LV00012B/1440